SCHAUM'S®
EASY OUTLINES

Probability
and Statistics

Online Diagnostic Test

Go to **Schaums.com** to launch the Schaum's Diagnostic Test.

This convenient application provides a 30-question multiple-choice test that will pinpoint areas of strength and weakness to help you focus your study. Questions cover all aspects of beginning chemistry, and the correct answers are explained in full. With a question-bank that rotates daily, the Schaum's Online Test also allows you to check your progress and readiness for final exams.

Other titles featured in Schaum's Online Diagnostic Test:

Schaum's Easy Outlines: Biochemistry
Schaum's Easy Outlines: Linear Algebra
Schaum's Easy Outlines: Molecular and Cell Biology
Schaum's Easy Outlines: Mathematical Handbook of Formulas
    and Tables
Schaum's Easy Outlines: Principles of Accounting
Schaum's Easy Outlines: Logic
Schaum's Easy Outlines: Bookkeeping and Accounting
Schaum's Easy Outlines: College Mathematics
Schaum's Easy Outlines: Applied Physics
Schaum's Easy Outlines: College Physics
Schaum's Easy Outlines: Differential Equations
Schaum's Easy Outlines: Basic Electricity
Schaum's Easy Outlines: Spanish, 2nd Edition
Schaum's Easy Outlines: French, 2nd Edition
Schaum's Easy Outlines: German, 2nd Edition
Schaum's Easy Outlines: Italian, 2nd Edition
Schaum's Easy Outlines: Writing and Grammar, 2nd Edition
Schaum's Easy Outlines: Geometry, 2nd Edition
Schaum's Easy Outlines: Calculus, 2nd Edition
Schaum's Easy Outlines: Statistics, 2nd Edition
Schaum's Easy Outlines: Elementary Algebra, 2nd Edition
Schaum's Easy Outlines: College Algebra, 2nd Edition
Schaum's Easy Outlines: Biology, 2nd Edition
Schaum's Easy Outlines: Human Anatomy and Physiology, 2nd Edition
Schaum's Easy Outlines: Organic Chemistry, 2nd Edition
Schaum's Easy Outlines: College Chemistry, 2nd Edition

SCHAUM'S®
EASY OUTLINES

Probability
and Statistics

Murray R. Spiegel, Ph.D.
John J. Schiller, Ph.D.
R. Alu Srinivasan, Ph.D.

Abridgement Editor:
Mike LeVan, Ph.D.

New York Chicago San Francisco Lisbon London Madrid Mexico City
Milan New Delhi San Juan Seoul Singapore Sydney Toronto

The *McGraw·Hill* Companies

The late **MURRAY R. SPIEGEL** an M.S. degree in Physics and a Ph.D. in Mathematics from Cornell University. He taught at Harvard, Columbia, and Rensselaer Polytechnic Institute, and worked at Oak Ridge as a mathematical consultant.

JOHN J. SCHILLER is an associate professor of Mathematics at Temple University. He received his Ph.D. from the University of Pennsylvania. He has published research papers in the area of Riemann surfaces, discrete mathematics, and mathematical biology. He has also coauthored several other mathematical texts.

R. ALU SRINIVASAN is a professor of Mathematics at Temple University. He received his Ph.D. from Wayne State University and has published extensively in probability and statistics.

MIKE LeVAN is associate professor and chair of the program of Mathematics at Transylvania University in Lexington, Kentucky. He received his B.S. from Eastern Kentucky University and both his Master of Applied Mathematics and Ph.D. degrees from Auburn University. He is the author or coauthor of several professional papers and was the winner in 2000 of the Bingham Award for Excellence in Teaching.

2 3 4 5 6 7 8 9 10 11 12 13 14 15   QVS/QVS   16 15 14

ISBN   978-0-07-177751-3
MHID   0-07-177751-2

Contents

Chapter 1
BASIC PROBABILITY

In This Chapter:

✔ *Random Experiments*
✔ *Sample Spaces*
✔ *Events*
✔ *The Concept of Probability*
✔ *The Axioms of Probability*
✔ *Some Important Theorems on Probability*
✔ *Assignment of Probabilities*
✔ *Conditional Probability*
✔ *Theorem on Conditional Probability*
✔ *Independent Events*
✔ *Bayes' Theorem or Rule*
✔ *Combinatorial Analysis*
✔ *Fundamental Principle of Counting*
✔ *Permutations*
✔ *Combinations*

1

✔ *Binomial Coefficients*
✔ *Stirling's Approximation to* n!

Random Experiments

We are all familiar with the importance of experiments in science and engineering. Experimentation is useful to us because we can assume that if we perform certain experiments under very nearly identical conditions, we will arrive at results that are essentially the same. In these circumstances, we are able to control the value of the variables that affect the outcome of the experiment.

However, in some experiments, we are not able to ascertain or control the value of certain variables so that the results will vary from one performance of the experiment to the next, even though most of the conditions are the same. These experiments are described as *random*. Here is an example:

Example 1.1. If we toss a die, the result of the experiment is that it will come up with one of the numbers in the set $\{1, 2, 3, 4, 5, 6\}$.

Sample Spaces

A set S that consists of all possible outcomes of a random experiment is called a *sample space*, and each outcome is called a *sample point*. Often there will be more than one sample space that can describe outcomes of an experiment, but there is usually only one that will provide the most information.

Example 1.2. If we toss a die, then one sample space is given by $\{1, 2, 3, 4, 5, 6\}$ while another is {even, odd}. It is clear, however, that the latter would not be adequate to determine, for example, whether an outcome is divisible by 3.

If is often useful to portray a sample space graphically. In such cases, it is desirable to use numbers in place of letters whenever possible.

If a sample space has a finite number of points, it is called a *finite sample space*. If it has as many points as there are natural numbers 1, 2, 3, ... , it is called a *countably infinite sample space*. If it has as many points as there are in some interval on the x axis, such as $0 \leq x \leq 1$, it is called a *noncountably infinite sample space*. A sample space that is finite or countably finite is often called a *discrete sample space*, while one that is noncountably infinite is called a *nondiscrete sample space*.

Example 1.3. The sample space resulting from tossing a die yields a discrete sample space. However, picking *any* number, not just integers, from 1 to 10, yields a nondiscrete sample space.

Events

An *event* is a subset A of the sample space S, i.e., it is a set of possible outcomes. If the outcome of an experiment is an element of A, we say that the event A *has occurred*. An event consisting of a single point of S is called a *simple* or *elementary event*.

As particular events, we have S itself, which is the *sure* or *certain event* since an element of S must occur, and the empty set $\varnothing$, which is called the *impossible event* because an element of $\varnothing$ cannot occur.

By using set operations on events in S, we can obtain other events in S. For example, if A and B are events, then

1. $A \cup B$ is the event "either A or B or both." $A \cup B$ is called the *union* of A and B.
2. $A \cap B$ is the event "both A and B." $A \cap B$ is called the *intersection* of A and B.
3. A' is the event "not A." A' is called the *complement* of A.
4. $A - B = A \cap B'$ is the event "A but not B." In particular, $A' = S - A$.

If the sets corresponding to events A and B are disjoint, i.e., $A \cap B = \varnothing$, we often say that the events are *mutually exclusive*. This means that they cannot both occur. We say that a collection of events $A_1, A_2, \dots , A_n$ is mutually exclusive if every pair in the collection is mutually exclusive.

The Concept of Probability

In any random experiment there is always uncertainty as to whether a particular event will or will not occur. As a measure of the *chance*, or *probability*, with which we can expect the event to occur, it is convenient to assign a number between 0 and 1. If we are sure or certain that an event will occur, we say that its probability is 100% or 1. If we are sure that the event will not occur, we say that its probability is zero. If, for example, the probability is $\frac{1}{4}$, we would say that there is a 25% chance it will occur and a 75% chance that it will not occur. Equivalently, we can say that the *odds* against occurrence are 75% to 25%, or 3 to 1.

There are two important procedures by means of which we can estimate the probability of an event.

1. **CLASSICAL APPROACH:** If an event can occur in h different ways out of a total of n possible ways, all of which are equally likely, then the probability of the event is h/n.
2. **FREQUENCY APPROACH:** If after n repetitions of an experiment, where n is very large, an event is observed to occur in h of these, then the probability of the event is h/n. This is also called the *empirical probability* of the event.

Both the classical and frequency approaches have serious drawbacks, the first because the words "equally likely" are vague and the second because the "large number" involved is vague. Because of these difficulties, mathematicians have been led to an *axiomatic approach* to probability.

The Axioms of Probability

Suppose we have a sample space S. If S is discrete, all subsets correspond to events and conversely; if S is nondiscrete, only special subsets (called *measurable*) correspond to events. To each event A in the class C of events, we associate a real number $P(A)$. The P is called a *probability function*, and $P(A)$ the *probability* of the event, if the following axioms are satisfied.

Axiom 1.   For every event A in class C,

$P(A) \geq 0$

Axiom 2.   For the sure or certain event S in the class C,

$P(S) = 1$

Axiom 3.   For any number of mutually exclusive events A_1, A_2, ...,
in the class C,

$P(A_1 \cup A_2 \cup \ldots) = P(A_1) + P(A_2) + \ldots$

In particular, for two mutually exclusive events A_1 and A_2,

$P(A_1 \cup A_2) = P(A_1) + P(A_2)$

Some Important Theorems on Probability

From the above axioms we can now prove various theorems on probability that are important in further work.

Theorem 1-1:   If $A_1 \subset A_2$, then   (1)

$P(A_1) \leq P(A_2)$ and $P(A_2 - A_1) = P(A_1) - P(A_2)$

Theorem 1-2:   For every event A,   (2)

$0 \leq P(A) \leq 1$,

i.e., a probability between 0 and 1.

Theorem 1-3:   For $\varnothing$, the empty set,   (3)

$P(\varnothing) = 0$

i.e., the impossible event has probability zero.

Theorem 1-4:   If A' is the complement of A, then   (4)

$P(A') = 1 - P(A)$

Theorem 1-5:   If $A = A_1 \cup A_2 \cup \ldots \cup A_n$, where $A_1, A_2, \ldots, A_n$ are
mutually exclusive events, then

$P(A) = P(A_1) + P(A_2) + \ldots + P(A_n)$ (5)

Theorem 1-6:   If A and B are any two events, then   (6)
$$P(A \cup B) = P(A) + P(B) - P(A \cap B)$$
More generally, if A_1, A_2, A_3 are any three events, then
$$P(A_1 \cup A_2 \cup A_3) = P(A_1) + P(A_2) + P(A_3) -$$
$$P(A_1 \cap A_2) - P(A_2 \cap A_3) - P(A_3 \cap A_1) +$$
$$P(A_1 \cap A_2 \cap A_3).$$
Generalizations to n events can also be made.

Theorem 1-7:   For any events A and B,   (7)
$$P(A) = P(A \cap B) + P(A \cap B')$$

Assignment of Probabilities

If a sample space S consists of a finite number of outcomes a_1, a_2, ... , a_n, then by Theorem 1-5,

$$P(A_1) + P(A_2) + ... + P(A_n) = 1 \tag{8}$$

where A_1, A_2, ... , A_n are elementary events given by $A_i = \{a_i\}$.

It follows that we can arbitrarily choose any nonnegative numbers for the probabilities of these simple events as long as the previous equation is satisfied. In particular, if we assume *equal probabilities* for all simple events, then

$$P(A_k) = \frac{1}{n}, \qquad k = 1, 2, ... , n \tag{9}$$

And if A is any event made up of h such simple events, we have

$$P(A) = \frac{h}{n} \tag{10}$$

This is equivalent to the classical approach to probability. We could of course use other procedures for assigning probabilities, such as frequency approach.

Assigning probabilities provides a *mathematical model*, the success of which must be tested by experiment in much the same manner that the theories in physics or others sciences must be tested by experiment.

Remember

The probability for any event must be between 0 and 1.

Conditional Probability

Let A and B be two events such that $P(A) > 0$. Denote $P(B \mid A)$ the probability of B *given that* A has occurred. Since A is known to have occurred, it becomes the new sample space replacing the original S. From this we are led to the definition

$$P(B \mid A) \equiv \frac{P(A \cap B)}{P(A)} \qquad (11)$$

or

$$P(A \cap B) \equiv P(A)P(B \mid A) \qquad (12)$$

In words, this is saying that the probability that both A and B occur is equal to the probability that A occurs times the probability that B occurs given that A has occurred. We call $P(B \mid A)$ the *conditional probability* of B given A, i.e., the probability that B will occur given that A has occurred. It is easy to show that conditional probability satisfies the axioms of probability previously discussed.

Theorem on Conditional Probability

Theorem 1-8: For any three events A_1, A_2, A_3, we have

$$P(A_1 \cap A_2 \cap A_3) = P(A_1)P(A_2 \mid A_1)P(A_3 \mid A_1 \cap A_2) \qquad (13)$$

In words, the probability that A_1 and A_2 and A_3 all occur is equal to the probability that A_1 occurs times the probability that A_2 occurs given that A_1 has occurred times the probability that A_3 occurs given that both A_1 and A_2 have occurred. The result is easily generalized to n events.

Theorem 1-9: If an event A must result in one of the mutually exclusive events A_1 , A_2 , ... , A_n , then $P(A)$

$$= P(A_1)P(A \mid A_1) + P(A_2)P(A \mid A_2) + ...$$
$$+ P(A_n)P(A \mid A_n) \tag{14}$$

Independent Events

If $P(B \mid A) = P(B)$, i.e., the probability of B occurring is not affected by the occurrence or nonoccurrence of A, then we say that A and B are *independent events*. This is equivalent to

$$P(A \cap B) = P(A)P(B) \tag{15}$$

Notice also that if this equation holds, then A and B are independent.

We say that three events $A1, A2, A3$ are *independent* if they are pairwise independent.

$$P(A_j \cap A_k) = P(A_j)P(A_k) \, j \neq k \qquad \text{where} \qquad j,k = 1,2,3 \tag{16}$$

and

$$P(A_1 \cap A_2 \cap A_3) = P(A_1)P(A_2)P(A_3) \tag{17}$$

Both of these properties must hold in order for the events to be independent. Independence of more than three events is easily defined.

Note!

In order to use this multiplication rule, all of your events must be independent.

Bayes' Theorem or Rule

Suppose that $A_1, A_2, \ldots, A_n$ are mutually exclusive events whose union is the sample space S, i.e., one of the events must occur. Then if A is any event, we have the important theorem:

Theorem 1-10 (Bayes' Rule):

$$P(A_k \mid A) = \frac{P(A_k)P(A \mid A_k)}{\sum_{j=1}^{n} P(A_j)P(A \mid A_j)} \qquad (18)$$

This enables us to find the probabilities of the various events A_1, $A_2, \ldots, A_n$ that can occur. For this reason Bayes' theorem is often referred to as a *theorem on the probability of causes*.

Combinatorial Analysis

In many cases the number of sample points in a sample space is not very large, and so direct enumeration or counting of sample points needed to obtain probabilities is not difficult. However, problems arise where direct counting becomes a practical impos-
sibility. In such cases use is made of *combinatorial analysis*, which could also be called a *sophisticated way of counting*.

Fundamental Principle of Counting

If one thing can be accomplished n_1 different ways and after this a second thing can be accomplished n_2 different ways, ... , and finally a kth thing can be accomplished in n_k different ways, then all k things can be accomplished in the specified order in $n_1 n_2 ... n_k$ different ways.

Permutations

Suppose that we are given n distinct objects and wish to *arrange r* of these objects in a line. Since there are n ways of choosing the first object, and after this is done, $n - 1$ ways of choosing the second object, ... , and finally $n - r + 1$ ways of choosing the rth object, it follows by the fundamental principle of counting that the number of different *arrangements*, or *permutations* as they are often called, is given by

$$_nP_r = n(n-1)...(n-r+1) \qquad (19)$$

where it is noted that the product has r factors. We call $_nP_r$ the *number of permutations of n objects taken r at a time.*

Example 1.4. It is required to seat 5 men and 4 women in a row so that the women occupy the even places. How many such arrangements are possible?

The men may be seated in $_5P_5$ ways, and the women $_4P_4$ ways. Each arrangement of the men may be associated with each arrangement of the women. Hence,

Number of arrangements = $_5P_5, _4P_4 = 5!\ 4! = (120)(24) = 2880$

In the particular case when $r = n$, this becomes

$$_nP_n = n(n-1)(n-2)...1 = n! \qquad (20)$$

which is called *n factorial*. We can write this formula in terms of factorials as

$$_nP_r = \frac{n!}{(n-r)!} \tag{21}$$

If $r = n$, we see that the two previous equations agree only if we have $0! = 1$, and we shall actually take this as the definition of $0!$.

Suppose that a set consists of n objects of which n_1 are of one type (i.e., indistinguishable from each other), n_2 are of a second type, ... , n_k are of a kth type. Here, of course, $n = n_1 + n_2 + ... + n_k$. Then the number of different permutations of the objects is

$$_nP_{n_1,n_2,...,n_k} = \frac{n!}{n_1!n_2!\cdots n_k!} \tag{22}$$

Combinations

In a permutation we are interested in the order of arrangements of the objects. For example, *abc* is a different permutation from *bca*. In many problems, however, we are only interested in selecting or choosing objects without regard to order. Such selections are called *combinations*. For example, *abc* and *bca* are the same combination.

The total number of combinations of r objects selected from n (also called the *combinations of n things taken r at a time*) is denoted by $_nC_r$ or $\binom{n}{r}$. We have

$$\binom{n}{r} = _nC_r = \frac{n!}{r!(n-r)!} \tag{23}$$

It can also be written

$$\binom{n}{r} = \frac{n(n-1)\cdots(n-r+1)}{r!} = \frac{_nP_r}{r!} \tag{24}$$

It is easy to show that

$$\binom{n}{r} = \binom{n}{n-r} \quad \text{or} \quad {}_nC_r = {}_nC_{n-r} \tag{25}$$

Example 1.5. From 7 consonants and 5 vowels, how many words can be formed consisting of 4 different consonants and 3 different vowels? The words need not have meaning.

The four different consonants can be selected in ${}_7C_4$ ways, the three different vowels can be selected in ${}_5C_3$ ways, and the resulting 7 different letters can then be arranged among themselves in ${}_7P_7 = 7!$ ways. Then

$$\text{Number of words} = {}_7C_4 \cdot {}_5C_3 \cdot 7! = 35 \cdot 10 \cdot 5040 = 1,764,000$$

Binomial Coefficients

The numbers from the combinations formula are often called *binomial coefficients* because they arise in the *binomial expansion*

$$(x+y)^n = x^n + \binom{n}{1}x^{n-1}y + \binom{n}{2}x^{n-2}y^2 + \cdots + \binom{n}{n}y^n \tag{26}$$

Stirling's Approximation to *n*!

When n is large, a direct evaluation of $n!$ may be impractical. In such cases, use can be made of the approximate formula

$$n \sim \sqrt{2\pi n}\, n^n e^{-n} \tag{27}$$

where $e = 2.71828 \ldots$, which is the base of natural logarithms. The symbol $\sim$ means that the ratio of the left side to the right side approaches 1 as $n \to \infty$.

Computing technology has largely eclipsed the value of Stirling's formula for numerical computations, but the approximation remains valuable for theoretical estimates (see Appendix A).

Chapter 2
DESCRIPTIVE STATISTICS

Descriptive Statistics

When giving a report on a data set, it is useful to describe the data set with terms familiar to most people. Therefore, we shall develop widely accepted terms that can help describe a data set. We shall discuss ways to describe the center, spread, and shape of a given data set.

Measures of Central Tendency

A *measure of central tendency* gives a single value that acts as a representative or average of the values of all the outcomes of your experiment. The main measure of central tendency we will use is the *arithmetic mean*. While the mean is used the most, two other measures of central tendency are also employed. These are the *median* and the *mode*.

 **Note!**

There are many ways to measure the central tendency of a data set, with the most common being the *arithmetic mean*, the *median*, and the *mode*. Each has advantages and disadvantages, depending on the data and the intended purpose.

Mean

If we are given a set of n numbers, say $x_1, x_2, \ldots, x_n$, then the mean, usually denoted by $\bar{x}$ or μ, is given by

$$\bar{x} = \frac{x_1 + x_2 + \cdots x_n}{n} \qquad (1)$$

Example 2.1. Consider the following set of integers:

$$S = \{1, 2, 3, 4, 5, 6, 7, 8, 9\}$$

The mean, $\bar{x}$, of the set S is

$$\bar{x} = \frac{1+2+3+4+5+6+7+8+9}{9} = 5$$

Median

The *median* is that value x for which $P(X < x) \leq \frac{1}{2}$ and $P(X > x) \leq \frac{1}{2}$. In other words, the median is the value where half of the values of x_1, x_2, ... , x_n are larger than the median, and half of the values of x_1, x_2, ... , x_n are smaller than the median.

Example 2.2.   Consider the following set of integers:

$$S = \{1, 6, 3, 8, 2, 4, 9\}$$

If we want to find the median, we need to find the value, x, where half the values are above x and half the values are below x. Begin by ordering the list:

$$S = \{1, 2, 3, 4, 6, 8, 9\}$$

Notice that the value 4 has three scores below it and three scores above it. Therefore, the median, in this example, is 4.
In some instances, it is quite possible that the value of the median will not be one of your observed values.

Example 2.3.   Consider the following set of integers:

$$S = \{1, 2, 3, 4, 6, 8, 9, 12\}$$

Since the set is already ordered, we can skip that step, but if you notice, we don't have just one value in the middle of the list. Instead, we have two values, namely 4 and 6. Therefore, the median can be *any* number between 4 and 6. In most cases, the average of the two numbers is reported. So, the median for this set of integers is

$$\frac{4+6}{2} = 5$$

In general, if we have n ordered data points, and n is an odd number, then the median is the data point located exactly in the middle of the set. This can be found in location $\frac{n+1}{2}$ of your set. If n is an even number, then the median is the average of the two middle terms of the ordered set. These can be found in locations $\frac{n}{2}$ and $\frac{n}{2}+1$.

Mode

The *mode* of a data set is the value that occurs most often, or in other words, has the most probability of occurring. Sometimes we can have two, three, or more values that have relatively large probabilities of occurrence. In such cases, we say that the distribution is *bimodal, trimodal*, or *multimodal*, respectively.

Example 2.4. Consider the following rolls of a ten-sided die:

$$R = \{2, 8, 1, 9, 5, 2, 7, 2, 7, 9, 4, 7, 1, 5, 2\}$$

The number that appears the most is the number 2. It appears four times. Therefore, the mode for the set R is the number 2.

Note that if the number 7 had appeared one more time, it would have been present four times as well. In this case, we would have had a bimodal distribution, with 2 *and* 7 as the modes.

Measures of Dispersion

Consider the following two sets of integers:

$$S = \{5, 5, 5, 5, 5, 5\} \quad \text{and} \quad R = \{0, 0, 0, 10, 10, 10\}$$

If we calculated the mean for both S and R, we would get the number 5 both times. However, these are two vastly different data sets. Therefore we need another descriptive statistic besides a measure of central tendency, which we shall call a *measure of dispersion*. We shall measure the dispersion or *scatter* of the values of our data set about the mean of the data set. If the values tend to be concentrated near the mean, then this measure shall be small, while if the values of the data set tend to be distributed far from the mean, then the measure will be large. The two measures of dispersions that are usually used are called the *variance* and *standard deviation*.

Variance and Standard Deviation

A quantity of great importance in probability and statistics is called the *variance*. The variance, denoted by σ^2, for a set of n numbers $x_1, x_2, \ldots ,$ x_n, is given by

$$\sigma^2 = \frac{[(x_1 - \mu)^2 + (x_2 - \mu)^2 + \cdots + (x_n - \mu)^2]}{n} \tag{2}$$

The variance is a nonnegative number. The positive square root of the variance is called the *standard deviation*.

Example 2.5.   Find the variance and standard deviation for the following set of test scores:

$$T = \{75, 80, 82, 87, 96\}$$

Since we are measuring dispersion about the mean, we will need to find the mean for this data set.

$$\mu = \frac{75+80+82+87+96}{5} = 84$$

Using the mean, we can now find the variance.

$$\sigma^2 = \frac{[(75-84)^2 + (80-84)^2 + (82-84)^2 + (87-84)^2 + (96-84)^2]}{5}$$

Which leads to the following:

$$\sigma^2 = \frac{[(81)+(16)+(4)+(9)+(144)]}{5} = 50.8$$

Therefore, the variance for this set of test scores is 50.8. To get the standard deviation, denoted by σ, simply take the square root of the variance.

$$\sigma = \sqrt{\sigma^2} = \sqrt{50.8} = 7.1274118$$

The variance and standard deviation are generally the most used quantities to report the measure of dispersion. However, there are other quantities that can also be reported.

You Need to Know

It is also widely accepted to divide the variance by ($n - 1$) as opposed to n. While this leads to a different result, as n gets large, the difference becomes minimal.

Percentiles

It is often convenient to subdivide your ordered data set by use of ordinates so that the amount of data points less than the ordinate is some percentage of the total amount of observations. The values corresponding to such areas are called *percentile values*, or briefly, *percentiles*. Thus, for example, the percentage of scores that fall below the ordinate at x_α is α. For instance, the amount of scores less than $x_{0.10}$ would be 0.10 or 10%, and $x_{0.10}$ would be called the *10th percentile*. Another example is the median. Since half the data points fall below the median, it is the *50th percentile* (or *fifth decile*), and can be denoted by $x_{0.50}$.

The *25th percentile* is often thought of as the median of the scores *below* the median, and the *75th percentile* is often thought of as the median of the scores *above* the median. The 25th percentile is called the first quartile, while the 75th percentile is called the third quartile. As you can imagine, the median is also known as the second quartile.

Interquartile Range

Another measure of dispersion is the *interquartile range*. The interquartile range is defined to be the first quartile subtracted from the third quartile. In other words, $x_{0.75} - x_{0.25}$

Example 2.6. Find the interquartile range from the following set of golf scores:

$$S = \{67, 69, 70, 71, 74, 77, 78, 82, 89\}$$

Since we have nine data points, and the set is ordered, the median is located in position $\dfrac{9+1}{2}$, or the 5th position. That means that the median for this set is 74.

The first quartile, $x_{0.25}$, is the median of the scores below the fifth position. Since we have four scores, the median is the average of the second and third score, which leads us to $x_{0.25} = 69.5$.

The third quartile, $x_{0.75}$, is the median of the scores above the fifth position. Since we have four scores, the median is the average of the seventh and eighth score, which leads us to $x_{0.75} = 80$.

Finally, the interquartile range is $x_{0.75} - x_{0.25} = 80 - 69.5 = 11.5$.

One final measure of dispersion that is worth mentioning is the *semiinterquartile range*. As the name suggests, this is simply half of the interquartile range.

Example 2.7. Find the semiinterquartile range for the previous data set.

$$\frac{1}{2}(x_{0.75} - x_{0.25}) = \frac{1}{2}(80 - 69.5) = 5.75$$

Skewness

The final descriptive statistics we will address in this section deals with the distribution of scores in your data set. For instance, you might have a symmetrical data set, or a data set that is evenly distributed, or a data set with more high values than low values.

Often a distribution is not symmetric about any value, but instead has a few more higher values, or a few more lower values. If the data set has a few more higher values, then it is said to be *skewed to the right*.

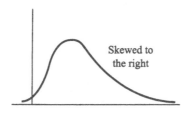

Figure 2-1
Skewed to the right.

If the data set has a few more lower values, then it is said to be skewed to the left.

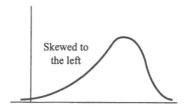

Figure 2-2
Skewed to the left.

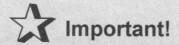 **Important!**

If a data set is skewed to the right or to the left, then there is a greater chance that an outlier may be in your data set. Outliers can greatly affect the mean and standard deviation of a data set. So, if your data set is skewed, you might want to think about using different measures of central tendency and dispersion!

Chapter 3
DISCRETE RANDOM VARIABLES

IN THIS CHAPTER:

✔ *Random Variables*
✔ *Discrete Probability Distribution*
✔ *Distribution Functions for Random Variables*
✔ *Distribution Functions for Discrete Random Variables*
✔ *Expected Values*
✔ *Variance and Standard Deviation*
✔ *Some Theorems on Expectation*
✔ *Some Theorems on Variance*

Random Variables

Suppose that to each point of a sample space we assign a number. We then have a *function* defined on the sample space. This function is called a *random variable* (or *stochastic variable*) or more precisely, a *random function* (*stochastic function*). It is usually denoted by a capital letter such as X or Y. In general, a random variable has some specified physical, geometrical, or other significance.

A random variable that takes on a finite or countably infinite number of values is called a *discrete random variable* while one that takes on a noncountably infinite number of values is called a *nondiscrete random variable*.

Discrete Probability Distribution

Let X be a discrete random variable, and suppose that the possible values that it can assume are given by $x_1, x_2, x_3, \ldots$, arranged in some order. Suppose also that these values are assumed with probabilities given by

$$P(X = x_k) = f(x_k) \qquad k = 1, 2, \ldots \tag{1}$$

It is convenient to introduce the *probability function*, also referred to as *probability distribution*, given by

$$P(X = x) = f(x) \tag{2}$$

For $x = x_k$, this reduces to our previous equation, while for other values of x, $f(x) = 0$.

In general, $f(x)$ is a probability function if

1. $f(x) \geq 0$
2. $\sum_x f(x) = 1$

where the sum in the second property above is taken over all possible values of x.

Example 3.1.   Suppose that a coin is tossed twice. Let X represent the number of heads that can come up. With each sample point we can associate a number for X as follows:

Sample Point	HH	HT	TH	TT
X	2	1	1	0

Now we can find the probability function corresponding to the random variable X. Assuming the coin is fair, we have

$$P(HH) = \frac{1}{4} \quad P(HT) = \frac{1}{4} \quad P(TH) = \frac{1}{4} \quad P(TT) = \frac{1}{4}$$

Then

$$P(X = 0) = P(TT) = \frac{1}{4}$$

$$P(X = 1) = P(HT \cup TH) = P(HT) + P(TH) = \frac{1}{4} + \frac{1}{4} = \frac{1}{2}$$

$$P(X = 2) = P(HH) = \frac{1}{4}$$

Thus, the probability function is given by

x	0	1	2
$f(x)$	1/4	1/2	1/4

Distribution Functions for Random Variables

The *cumulative distribution function*, or briefly the *distribution function*, for a random variable X is defined by

$$F(x) = P(X \le x) \qquad (3)$$

where x is any real number, i.e., $-\infty \le x \le \infty$.

In words, the cumulative distribution function will determine the probability that the random variable will take on *any* value x or less.

The distribution function $F(x)$ has the following properties:

1. $F(x)$ is nondecreasing [i.e., $F(x) \le F(y)$ if $x \le y$].
2. $\lim\limits_{x \to -\infty} F(x) = 0; \quad \lim\limits_{x \to \infty} F(x) = 1$
3. $F(x)$ is continuous from the right [i.e., $\lim\limits_{x \to 0^+} F(x+h) = F(x)$ for all x].

Distribution Functions for Discrete Random Variables

The distribution function for a discrete random variable X can be obtained from its probability function by noting that, for all x in $(-\infty, \infty)$,

$$F(x) = \begin{cases} 0 & -\infty < x < x_1 \\ f(x_1) & x_1 \le x < x_2 \\ f(x_1) + f(x_2) & x_2 \le x < x_3 \\ \vdots & \vdots \\ f(x_1) + \cdots f(x_n) & x_n \le x < \infty \end{cases} \qquad (4)$$

It is clear that the probability function of a discrete random variable can be obtained from the distribution function noting that

$$f(x) = F(x) - \lim_{u \to x^-} F(u) \qquad (5)$$

Expected Values

A very important concept in probability and statistics is that of *mathematical expectation, expected value*, or briefly the *expectation*, of a random variable. For a discrete random variable X having the possible values $x_1, x_2, ..., x_n$, the expectation of X is defined as

$$E(X) = x_1 P(X = x_1) + \cdots + x_n P(X = x_n) = \sum_{j=1}^{n} x_j P(X = x_j) \qquad (6)$$

or equivalently, if $P(x = x_j) = f(x_j)$,

$$E(X) = x_1 f(x_1) + \cdots + x_n f(x_n) = \sum_{j=1}^{n} x_j f(x_j) = \sum_x x f(x) \qquad (7)$$

where the last summation is taken over all appropriate values of x.

Notice that when the probabilities are all equal,

$$E(X) = \frac{x_1 + x_2 + \cdots x_n}{n} \qquad (8)$$

which is simply the mean of $x_1, x_2, ..., x_n$.

Example 3.2. Suppose that a game is to be played with a single die assumed fair. In this game a player wins \$20 if a 2 turns up; \$40 if a 4 turns up; loses \$30 if a 6 turns up; while the player neither wins nor loses if any other face turns up. Find the expected sum of money to be won.

Let X be the random variable giving the amount of money won on any toss. The possible amounts won when the die turns up 1, 2, ..., 6 are $x_1, x_2, ..., x_6$, respectively, while the probabilities of these are $f(x_1)$, $f(x_2), ..., f(x_6)$. The probability function for X is given by:

x	0	+20	0	+40	0	−30
$f(x)$	1/6	1/6	1/6	1/6	1/6	1/6

Therefore, the expected value, or expectation, is

$$E(X) = (0)\left(\frac{1}{6}\right) + (20)\left(\frac{1}{6}\right) + (0)\left(\frac{1}{6}\right) + (40)\left(\frac{1}{6}\right) + (0)\left(\frac{1}{6}\right) + (-30)\left(\frac{1}{6}\right) = 5$$

It follows that the player can expect to win $5. In a fair game, therefore, the player should expect to pay $5 in order to play the game.

Remember

The expected value of a discrete random variable is its measure of central tendency!

Variance and Standard Deviation

We have already noted that the expectation of a random variable X is often called the *mean* and can be denoted by μ. As we noted in Chapter Two, another quantity of great importance in probability and statistics is the *variance*. If X is a discrete random variable taking the values x_1, x_2, ..., x_n, and having probability function $f(x)$, then the variance is given by

$$\sigma_X^2 = E\left[(X - \mu)^2\right] = \sum_{j=1}^{n}(x_j - \mu)^2 f(x_j) = \sum_x (x - \mu)^2 f(x) \qquad (9)$$

In the special case where all the probabilities are equal, we have

$$\sigma_X^2 = \frac{(x_1 - \mu)^2 + (x_2 - \mu)^2 + \cdots + (x_n - \mu)^2}{n} \qquad (10)$$

which is the variance we found for a set of n numbers values x_1, x_2, $\dots$, x_n.

Example 3.3.   Find the variance for the game played in Example 3.2.

Recall the probability function for the game:

x_j	0	+20	0	+40	0	−30
$f(x_j)$	1/6	1/6	1/6	1/6	1/6	1/6

We have already found the mean to be $\mu = 5$, therefore, the variance is given by

$$\sigma_X^2 = (0-5)^2 \left(\frac{1}{6}\right) + (20-5)^2 \left(\frac{1}{6}\right) + (0-5)^2 \left(\frac{1}{6}\right) + (40-5)^2 \left(\frac{1}{6}\right)$$
$$+ (0-5)^2 \left(\frac{1}{6}\right) + (-30-5)^2 \left(\frac{1}{6}\right) = \frac{2750}{6} = 458.33\bar{3}$$

The standard deviation can be found by simply taking the square root of the variance. Therefore, the standard deviation is

$$\sigma_X = \sqrt{458.33\bar{3}} = 21.40872096$$

Notice that if X has certain *dimensions* or *units*, such as *centimeters* (cm), then the variance of X has units cm^2 while the standard deviation has the same unit as X, i.e., cm. It is for this reason that the standard deviation is often used.

Some Theorems on Expectation

Theorem 3-1: If c is any constant, then
$$E(cX) = cE(X) \qquad (11)$$

Theorem 3-2: If X and Y are any random variables, then
$$E(X + Y) = E(X) + E(Y) \qquad (12)$$

Theorem 3-3: If X and Y are independent random variables, then
$$E(XY) = E(X)E(Y) \qquad (13)$$

 **Note!**

These properties hold for *any* random variable, not just discrete random variables. We will examine another type of random variable in the next chapter.

Some Theorems on Variance

Theorem 3-4:
$$\sigma^2 = E[(X - \mu)^2] = E(X^2) - \mu^2 = E(X^2) - [E(X)]^2 \qquad (14)$$

where $\mu = E(X)$.

Theorem 3-5:   If c is any constant,

$$Var(cX) = c^2 Var(X) \qquad (15)$$

Theorem 3-6:   The quantity $E[(X - a)^2]$ is a minimum when (16)

$$a = \mu = E(X)$$

Theorem 3-7:   If X and Y are independent random variables,

$$Var(X + Y) = Var(X) + Var(Y) \quad \text{or} \quad \sigma^2_{X+Y} = \sigma^2_X + \sigma^2_Y \qquad (17)$$
$$Var(X - Y) = Var(X) + Var(Y) \quad \text{or} \quad \sigma^2_{X-Y} = \sigma^2_X + \sigma^2_Y$$

Don't Forget

These theorems apply to the variance and not to the standard deviation! Make sure you convert your standard deviation into variance before you apply these theorems.

Generalizations of Theorem 3-7 to more than two independent random variables are easily made. In words, the variance of a sum of independent variables equals the sum of their variances.

Again, these theorems hold true for discrete and nondiscrete random variables.

Example 3.4. Let X and Y be the random independent events of rolling a fair die. Compute the expected value of $X + Y$, and the variance of $X + Y$.

The following is the probability function for X and Y, individually:

x_j	1	2	3	4	5	6
$f(x_j)$	1/6	1/6	1/6	1/6	1/6	1/6

From this, we get the following:

$$\mu_X = \mu_Y = 3.5 \quad \text{and} \quad \sigma_X^2 = \sigma_Y^2 = 2.91\overline{666}$$

There are two ways we could compute $E(X + Y)$ and $Var(X + Y)$. First, we could compute the probability distribution of $X + Y$, and find the expected value and variance from there. Notice that the possible values for $X + Y$ are 2, 3, ..., 11, 12.

$x + y$	2	3	4	5	6
$f(x + y)$	1/36	2/36	3/36	4/36	5/36

$x + y$	7	8	9	10	11	12
$f(x + y)$	6/36	5/36	4/36	3/36	2/36	1/36

We can find the expected value as follows:

$$E(X+Y) = (2)\left(\frac{1}{36}\right) + (3)\left(\frac{2}{36}\right) + \cdots + (11)\left(\frac{2}{36}\right) + (12)\left(\frac{1}{36}\right) = \frac{252}{36} = 7$$

It then follows that the variance is:

$$Var(X+Y) = \left[(2-7)^2\left(\frac{1}{36}\right) + \cdots (12-7)^2\left(\frac{1}{36}\right)\right] = \frac{210}{36} = 5.83\overline{33}$$

However, using Theorems 3-2 and 3-7 makes this an easy task.

By using Theorem 3-2,

$$E(X + Y) = E(X) + E(Y) = 3.5 + 3.5 = 7.$$

By using Theorem 3-7,

$$Var(X + Y) = Var(X) + Var(Y) = 2.91\overline{666} + 2.91\overline{666} = 5.83\overline{33}$$

Since $X = Y$, we could have also found the expected value using Theorems 3-1:

$$E(X + Y) = E(X + X) = E(2X) = 2[E(X)] = 2(3.5) = 7$$

However, we could *not* have used Theorem 3-5 to find the variance because we are basically using the same distribution, X, twice, and X is not independent from itself. Notice that we get the wrong variance when we apply the theorem:

$$Var(X + X) = Var(2X) = \left(2^2\right)Var(X) = 4Var(X) = 11.6\overline{66}$$

Chapter 4
CONTINUOUS RANDOM VARIABLES

IN THIS CHAPTER:

✔ *Continuous Random Variables*
✔ *Continuous Probability Distribution*
✔ *Distribution Functions for Continuous Random Variables*
✔ *Expected Values*
✔ *Variance*
✔ *Properties of Expected Values and Variances*
✔ *Graphical Interpretations*

Continuous Random Variables

A nondiscrete random variable X is said to be *absolutely continuous*, or simply *continuous*, if its distribution function may be represented as

$$F(x) = P(X \le x) = \int\limits_{-\infty}^{x} f(u)\, du \qquad (1)$$

where the function $f(x)$ has the properties

1. $f(x) \ge 0$

2. $\int\limits_{-\infty}^{\infty} f(x)\, dx = 1$

Continuous Probability Distribution

It follows from the above that if X is a continuous random variable, then the probability that X takes on any one particular value is zero, whereas the *interval probability* that X lies *between two different values*, say a and b, is given by

$$P(a < X < b) = \int\limits_{b}^{a} f(x)\, dx \qquad (2)$$

Example 4.1. If an individual were selected at random from a large group of adult males, the probability that his height X is precisely 68 inches (i.e., 68.000... inches) would be zero. However, there is a probability greater than zero that X is between 67.000... inches and 68.000... inches.

A function $f(x)$ that satisfies the above requirements is called a *probability function* or *probability distribution* for a continuous random variable, but it is more often called a *probability density function* or simply *density function*. Any function $f(x)$ satisfying the two properties above will automatically be a density function, and required probabilities can be obtained from (2).

Example 4.2.   Find the constant c such that the function

$$f(x) = \begin{cases} cx^2 & 0 < x < 3 \\ 0 & otherwise \end{cases}$$

is a density function, and then find $P(1 < X < 2)$.

Notice that if $c \geq 0$, then Property 1 is satisfied. So $f(x)$ must satisfy Property 2 in order for it to be a density function. Now

$$\int_{-\infty}^{\infty} f(x)\,dx = \int_{0}^{3} cx^2\,dx = \frac{cx^3}{3}\Big|_0^3 = 9c$$

and since this must equal 1, we have $c = \frac{1}{9}$, and our density function is

$$f(x) = \begin{cases} \dfrac{1}{9}x^2 & 0 < x < 3 \\[2mm] 0 & otherwise \end{cases}$$

Next,

$$P(1 < X < 2) = \int_{1}^{2} \frac{1}{9}x^2\,dx = \frac{x^3}{27}\Big|_1^2 = \frac{8}{27} - \frac{1}{27} = \frac{7}{27}$$

Distribution Functions for Continuous Random Variables

Recall the cumulative distribution function, or distribution function, for a random variable is defined by

$$F(x) = P(X \le x) \tag{3}$$

where x is any real number, i.e., $-\infty \le x \le \infty$. So,

$$F(x) = \int_{-\infty}^{x} f(x)\, dx \tag{4}$$

Example 4.3. Find the distribution function for example 4.2.

$$F(x) = \int_{-\infty}^{x} f(x)\, dx = \int_{0}^{x} \frac{1}{9} x^2 \, dx = \frac{x^3}{27}$$

where $x \le 3$.

There is a nice relationship between the distribution function and the density function. To see this relationship, consider the probability that a random variable X takes on a value, x, and a value fairly close to x, say $x + \Delta x$.

The probability that X is between x and $x + \Delta x$ is given by

$$P(x \le X \le x + \Delta x) = \int_{x}^{x+\Delta x} f(u)\, du \tag{5}$$

so that if Δx is small, we have approximately

$$P(x \le X \le x + \Delta x) + f(x)\Delta x \tag{6}$$

We also see from (1) on differentiating both sides that

$$\frac{dF(x)}{dx} = f(x) \tag{7}$$

at all points where $f(x)$ is continuous, i.e., the derivative of the distribution function is the density function.

Expected Values

If X is a continuous random variable having probability density function $f(x)$, then it can be shown that

$$E[g(x)] = \int_{-\infty}^{\infty} g(x) f(x) dx \qquad (8)$$

Example 4.4.   The density function of a random X is given by

$$f(x) = \begin{cases} \dfrac{1}{2}x & 0 < x < 2 \\ \\ 0 & \text{otherwise} \end{cases}$$

The expected value of X is then

$$E(X) = \int_{-\infty}^{\infty} x\, f(x)\, dx = \int_{0}^{2} x\left(\frac{1}{2}x\right) dx = \int_{0}^{2} \frac{x^2}{2}\, dx = \frac{x^3}{6}\bigg|_{0}^{2} = \frac{4}{3}$$

Variance

If X is a continuous random variable having probability density function $f(x)$, then the variance is given by

$$\sigma_X^2 = E\left[(X - \mu)^2\right] = \int_{-\infty}^{\infty} (x - \mu)^2\, f(x)\, dx \qquad (9)$$

provided that the integral converges.

Example 4.5.   Find the variance and standard deviation of the random variable from Example 4.4, using the fact that the mean was found to be $\mu = E(X) = \dfrac{4}{3}$.

$$\sigma^2 = E\left[\left(X - \frac{4}{3}\right)^2\right] = \int_{-\infty}^{\infty}\left(x - \frac{4}{3}\right)^2 f(x)\,dx = \int_{-\infty}^{\infty}\left(x - \frac{4}{3}\right)^2\left(\frac{1}{2}x\right)dx = \frac{2}{9}$$

and so the standard deviation is $\sigma = \sqrt{\dfrac{2}{9}} = \dfrac{\sqrt{2}}{3}$.

Recall that the variance (or standard deviation) is a measure of the *dispersion*, or *scatter*, of the values of the random variable about the mean μ. If the values tend to be concentrated near the mean, the variance is small; while if the values tend to be distributed far from the mean, the variance is large. The situation is indicated graphically in Figure 4-1 for the case of two continuous distributions having the same mean μ.

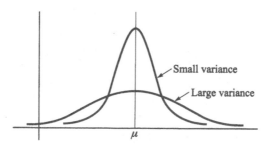

Figure 4-1

Properties of Expected Values and Variances

In Chapter Three, we discussed several theorems that applied to expected values and variances of random variables. Since these theorems apply to any random variable, we can apply them to continuous random variables as well as their discrete counterparts.

Example 4.6. Given the probability density function in Example 4.4, find $E(3X)$ and $Var(3X)$.

Using our the direct computational method,

$$E(3X) = \int_{-\infty}^{\infty} 3x\, f(x)\, dx = \int_{0}^{2} 3x\left(\frac{1}{2}x\right) dx = \int_{0}^{2} \frac{3}{2}x^2\, dx = \frac{x^3}{2}\bigg|_{0}^{2} = 4$$

Using Theorems 3-1 and 3-2, respectively, we could have found these much easier as follows:

$$E(3X) = 3E(X) = 3\left(\frac{4}{3}\right) = 4$$

or

$$E(3X) = E(X + X + X) = E(X) + E(X) + E(X) = \frac{4}{3} + \frac{4}{3} + \frac{4}{3} = 4$$

Using Theorem 3-5, the variance is also quite simple to find:

$$Var(3X) = 3^2\, Var(X) = 9\left(\frac{2}{9}\right) = 2$$

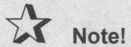 **Note!**

These theorems aren't just for show! They can make your work much easier, so learn them and take advantage of them.

Graphical Interpretations

If $f(x)$ is the density function for a random variable X, then we can represent $y = f(x)$ by a curve, as seen below in Figure 4-2. Since $f(x) \geq 0$, the curve cannot fall below the x-axis. The entire area bounded by the curve and the x-axis must be 1 because of property 2 listed above. Geometrically, the probability that X is between a and b, i.e., $P(a < X < b)$, is then represented by the area shown shaded, in Figure 4-2.

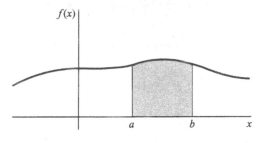

Figure 4-2

The distribution function $F(x) = P(X \leq x)$ is a monotonically increasing function that increases from 0 to 1 and is represented by a curve as in the following figure:

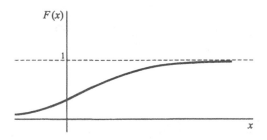

Figure 4-3

Chapter 5
EXAMPLES OF RANDOM VARIABLES

IN THIS CHAPTER:

✔ *Binomial Distribution*
✔ *Properties of Binomial Distributions*
✔ *The Normal Distribution*
✔ *Examples of the Normal Distribution*
✔ *Poisson Distributions*
✔ *Relationships between Binomial and Normal Distributions*
✔ *Relationships between Binomial and Poisson Distributions*
✔ *Relationships between Poisson and Normal Distributions*
✔ *Central Limit Theorem*
✔ *Law of Large Numbers*

Binomial Distribution

Suppose that we have an experiment such as tossing a coin or die repeatedly or choosing a marble from an urn repeatedly. Each toss or selection is called a *trial*. In any single trial there will be a probability associated with a particular event such as head on the coin, four on the die, or selection of a specific color marble. In some cases this probability will not change from one trial to the next (as in tossing  a coin or die). Such trials are then said to be *independent* and are often called *Bernoulli trials* after James Bernoulli who investigated them at the end of the seventeenth century.

Let p be the probability that an event will happen in any single Bernoulli trial (called the *probability of success*). Then $q = 1 - p$ is the probability that the event will fail to happen in any single trial (called the *probability of failure*). The probability that the event will happen exactly x times in n trials (i.e., x successes and $n - x$ failures will occur) is given by the probability function

$$f(x) = P(X = x) = \binom{n}{x} p^x q^{n-x} = \frac{n!}{x!(n-x)!} p^x q^{n-x} \qquad (1)$$

where the random variable X denotes the number of successes in n trials and $x = 0, 1, \ldots, n$.

Example 5.1.   The probability of getting exactly 2 heads in 6 tosses of a fair coin is

$$P(X = 2) = \binom{6}{2}\left(\frac{1}{2}\right)^2\left(\frac{1}{2}\right)^{6-2} = \frac{6!}{2!\,4!}\left(\frac{1}{2}\right)^2\left(\frac{1}{2}\right)^4 = \frac{15}{64}$$

The discrete probability function $f(x)$ is often called the *binomial distribution* since $x = 0, 1, 2, \ldots, n$, it corresponds to successive terms in the *binomial expansion*

$$(q+p)^n = q^n + \binom{n}{1}q^{n-1}p + \binom{n}{2}q^{n-2}p^2 + \cdots + p^n = \sum_{x=0}^{n}\binom{n}{x}p^x q^{n-x} \quad (2)$$

The special case of a binomial distribution with $n = 1$ is also called the *Bernoulli distribution.*

Properties of Binomial Distributions

As with other distributions, we would like to know the descriptive statistics for the binomial distribution. They are as follows:

Mean	$\mu = np$
Variance	$\sigma^2 = np\,(1-p)$
Standard Deviation	$\sigma = \sqrt{np(1-p)}$

Example 5.2.   Toss a fair coin 100 times, and count the number of heads that appear. Find the mean, variance, and standard deviation of this experiment.

In 100 tosses of a fair coin, the expected or mean number of heads is $\mu = (100)(0.5) = 50$.

The variance is found to be $\sigma^2 = (100)(0.5)(0.5) = 25$.

This means the standard deviation is $\sigma = \sqrt{(100)(0.5)(0.5)} = \sqrt{25} = 5$.

The Normal Distribution

One of the most important examples of a continuous probability distribution is the *normal distribution*, sometimes called the *Gaussian distribution*. The density function for this distribution is given by

$$f(x) = \frac{1}{\sigma\sqrt{2\pi}} e^{-(x-\mu)^2/2\sigma^2} \qquad -\infty < x < \infty \qquad (3)$$

where μ and σ are the mean and standard deviation, respectively. The corresponding distribution function is given by

$$F(x) = P(X \le x) = \frac{1}{\sigma\sqrt{2\pi}} \int_{-\infty}^{x} e^{-(v-\mu)^2/2\sigma^2} \, dv \qquad (4)$$

If X has the distribution function listed above, then we say that the random variable X is *normally distributed* with mean μ and variance σ^2. If we let Z be the random variable corresponding to the following

$$Z = \frac{X - \mu}{\sigma} \qquad (5)$$

then Z is called the *standard variable* corresponding to X. The mean or expected value of Z is 0 and the standard deviation is 1. In such cases the density function for Z can be obtained from the definition of a normal distribution by allowing $\mu = 0$ and $\sigma^2 = 1$, yielding

$$f(z) = \frac{1}{\sqrt{2\pi}} e^{-z^2/2} \qquad (6)$$

This is often referred to as the *standard normal density function*. The corresponding distribution function is given by

$$F(z) = P(Z \le z) = \frac{1}{\sqrt{2\pi}} \int_{-\infty}^{z} e^{-u^2/2} \, du = \frac{1}{2} + \frac{1}{\sqrt{2\pi}} \int_{0}^{z} e^{-u^2/2} \, du \quad (7)$$

We sometimes call the value z of the standardized variable Z the *standard score*.

A graph of the standard normal density function, sometimes called the *standard normal curve*, is shown in Figure 5-1. In this graph we have indicated the areas within 1, 2, and 3 standard deviations of the mean (i.e., between $z = -1$ and $+1$, $z = -2$ and $+2$, $z = -3$ and $+3$) as equal, respectively, to 68.27%, 95.45%, and 99.73% of the total area, which is one. This means that

$$P(-1 \le Z \le 1) = 0.6827$$
$$P(-2 \le Z \le 2) = 0.9545$$
$$P(-3 \le Z \le 3) = 0.9973$$

 **Note!**

The normal distribution is very important! It will quite often come up in practice, so make sure you understand how to use this distribution.

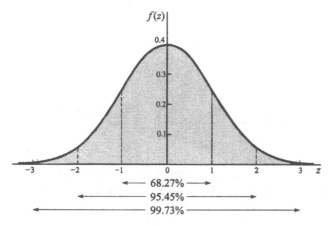

Figure 5-1

A table giving the areas under the curve bounded by the ordinates at $z = 0$ and any positive value of z is given in Appendix B. From this table the areas between any two ordinates can be found by using the symmetry of the curve about $z = 0$.

Examples of the Normal Distribution

Since this distribution is so important, we will now run through a few examples of how to use the distribution.

Example 5.3. Find the area under the standard normal curve between $z = 0$ and $z = 1.2$.

Using the table in Appendix B, proceed down the column marked z until entry 1.2 is reached. Then proceed right to column marked 0. The result, 0.3849, is the required area and represents the probability that Z is between 0 and 1.2. Therefore, $P(0 \le Z \le 1.2) = 0.3849$.

Example 5.4.   Find the area under the standard normal curve between $z = -0.46$ and $z = 2.21$.

Figure 5-2

Consider the following picture of the density curve.

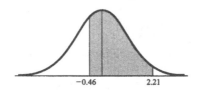

Figure 5-3

The required area can be broken down into two parts. First, the area between $z = -0.46$ and $z = 0$, and secondly, the area between $z = 0$ and $z = 0$ and $z = 2.21$.

Since the normal curve is symmetric, the area between $z = -0.46$ and $z = 0$ is the same as the area between $z = 0$ and $z = 0.46$. Using Appendix B, we can see that this area is 0.1772. In other words,

$$P(-0.46 \leq Z \leq 0 = P(0 \leq Z \leq 0.46) = 0.1772$$

Using Appendix B to find the area between $z = 0$ and $z = 2.21$ is found to be 0.4864. This means

$$P(0 \leq Z \leq 2.21) = 0.4864$$

This allows us to determine the required area as follows:

Total Area   =   (area between $z = -0.46$ and $z = 0$) +
                      (area between $z = 0$ and $z = 2.21$)
             = $0.1722 + 0.4864$
             = 0.6586

Therefore $P(-0.46 \leq Z \leq 2.21) = 0.6636$.

Example 5.5.   The mean weight of 500 male students at a certain college is 151 lb and the standard deviation is 15 lb. Assuming the weights are normally distributed, find how many students weigh (a) between 120 and 155 lb, (b) more than 185 lb.

(a) If weights are recorded to the nearest pound, then weights recorded as being between 120 and 155 lb can actually have any value from 119.5 to 155.5 lb.

We need to find the standard scores for 119.5 and 155.5.

119.5 lb in standard units   = $(119.5 - 151) / 15$
                               = -2.10

155.5 lb in standard units   = $(155.5 - 151) / 15$
                               = 0.30

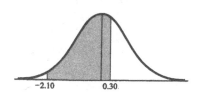

Figure 5-4

Required proportion of students

$=$ (area between $z = -2.10$ and $z = 0.30$)
$=$ (area between $z = -2.10$ and $z = 0$)
$+$ (area between $z = 0$ and $z = 0.30$)
$=$ $0.4821 + 0.1179$
$=$ 0.6000

This means that of the 500 male students polled, 60% of them weigh between 120 and 155 lb. Then the number of students in this range is $(500)(0.6000) = 300$.

(b) Notice that students weighing more than 185 lb must weigh at least 185.5 lb.

185.5 lb in standard units $=$ $(185.5 - 151) / 15$
$=$ 2.30

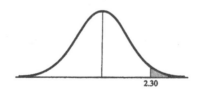

2.30

Figure 5-5

Required proportion of students

$=$ (area to the right of $z = 2.30$)
$=$ (area to the right of $z = 0$)
$-$ (area between $z = 0$ and $z = 2.30$)
$=$ $0.5 - 0.4893$
$=$ 0.0107

Then the number weighing more than 185 lb is $(500)(0.0107) = 5$.

If W denotes the weight of a student chosen at random, we can summarize the above results in terms of probability by writing

$$P(119.5 \le W \le 155.5 = 0.6000 \qquad P(W \ge 185.5) = 0.0107$$

Poisson Distributions

Let X be a discrete random variable that can take on the values 0, 1, 2,... such that the probability function of X is given by

$$f(x) = P(X = x) = \frac{\lambda^x e^{-\lambda}}{x!} \qquad x = 0, 1, 2, \ldots \qquad (8)$$

where λ is a given positive constant. This distribution is called the *Poisson distribution* (after S. D. Poisson, who discovered it in the early part of the nineteenth century), and a random variable having this distribution is said to be *Poisson distributed*.

The values of the Poisson distribution can be obtained by using Appendix F, which gives values of $e^{-\lambda}$ for various values of λ.

Example 5.6. If the probability that an individual will suffer a bad reaction from injection of a given serum is 0.001, determine the probability that out of 2000 individuals, (a) exactly 3, (b) more than 2, individuals will suffer a bad reaction.

Let X denote the number of individuals suffering a bad reaction. X is Bernoulli distributed, but since bad reactions are assumed to be rare events, we can suppose that X is Poisson distributed, i.e.,

$$P(X = x) = \frac{\lambda^x e^{-\lambda}}{x!} \qquad \text{where } \lambda = np = (2000)(0.001) = 2$$

(a)

$$P(X = 3) = \frac{2^3 e^{-2}}{3!} = 0.180$$

(b)

$$
\begin{aligned}
P(X > 2) &= 1 - \left[P(X = 0) + P(X = 1) + P(X = 2) \right] \\
&= 1 - \left[\frac{2^0 e^{-2}}{0!} + \frac{2^1 e^{-2}}{1!} + \frac{2^2 e^{-2}}{2!} \right] \\
&= 1 - 5e^{-2} \\
&= 0.323
\end{aligned}
$$

An exact evaluation of the probabilities using the binomial distribution would require much more labor.

Relationships between Binomial and Normal Distributions

If n is large and if neither p nor q is too close to zero, the binomial distribution can be closely approximated by a normal distribution with standardized random variable given by

$$Z = \frac{X - np}{\sqrt{npq}} \tag{9}$$

Here X is the random variable giving the number of successes in n Bernoulli trials and p is the probability of success. The approximation becomes better with increasing n and is exact in the limiting case. In practice, the approximation is very good if both np and nq are greater than 5. The fact that the binomial distribution approaches the normal distribution can be described by writing

$$\lim_{n \to \infty} P\left(a \le \frac{X - np}{\sqrt{npq}} \le b\right) = \frac{1}{\sqrt{2\pi}} \int_a^b e^{-u^2/2} \, du \qquad (10)$$

In words, we say that the standardized random variable $(X - np)/\sqrt{npq}$ is *asymptotically normal*.

Example 5.7.   Find the probability of getting between 3 and 6 heads inclusive in 10 tosses of a fair coin by using (a) the binomial distribution and (b) the normal approximation to the binomial distribution.

(a) Let X have the random variable giving the number of heads that will turn up in 10 tosses. Then

$$P(X = 3) = \binom{10}{3}\left(\frac{1}{2}\right)^3\left(\frac{1}{2}\right)^7 = \frac{15}{28} \qquad P(X = 4) = \binom{10}{4}\left(\frac{1}{2}\right)^4\left(\frac{1}{2}\right)^6 = \frac{105}{512}$$

$$P(X = 5) = \binom{10}{5}\left(\frac{1}{2}\right)^5\left(\frac{1}{2}\right)^5 = \frac{63}{256} \qquad P(X = 6) = \binom{10}{6}\left(\frac{1}{2}\right)^6\left(\frac{1}{2}\right)^4 = \frac{105}{512}$$

Then the required probability is

$$P(3 \le X \le 6) = \frac{15}{28} + \frac{105}{512} + \frac{63}{256} + \frac{105}{512} = 0.7734$$

(b) Treating the data as continuous, it follows that 3 to 6 heads can be considered 2.5 to 6.5 heads. Also, the mean and the variance for the binomial distribution is given by $\mu = np = (10)\left(\frac{1}{2}\right) = 5$ and

$$\sigma = \sqrt{npq} = \sqrt{(10)\left(\frac{1}{2}\right)\left(\frac{1}{2}\right)} = 1.58.$$

$$2.5 \text{ in standard units} = \frac{2.5 - 5}{1.58} = -1.58$$

$$6.5 \text{ in standard units} = \frac{6.5 - 5}{1.58} = 0.95$$

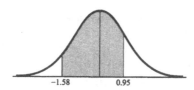

Figure 5-6

Required probability	=	(area between $z = -1.58$ and $z = 0.95$)
	=	(area between $z = -1.58$ and $z = 0$)
		+ (area between $z = 0$ and $z = 0.95$)
	=	0.4429 + 0.3289
	=	0.7718

which compares very well with the true value 0.7734 obtained in part (a). The accuracy is even better for larger values of n.

Relationships between Binomial and Poisson Distributions

In the binomial distribution, if n is large while the probability p of occurrence of an event is close to zero, so that $q = 1 - p$ is close to one, the event is called a *rare event*. In practice, we shall consider an event as rare if the number of trials is at least 50 ($n \geq 50$) while np is less than 5. For such cases, the binomial distribution is very closely approximated by the Poisson distribution with $\lambda = np$. This is to be expected on comparing the equations for the means and variances for both distributions. By substituting $\lambda = np$, $q \approx 1$ and $p \approx 0$ into the equations for the mean and variance of a binomial distribution, we get the results for the mean and variance for the Poisson distribution.

Relationships between Poisson and Normal Distributions

Since there is a relationship between the binomial and normal distributions and between the binomial and Poisson distributions, we would expect that there should be a relation between the Poisson and normal distributions. This is in fact the case. We can show that if X is the following Poisson random variable

$$f(x) = \frac{\lambda^x e^{-\lambda}}{x!} \tag{11}$$

and

$$\frac{X - \lambda}{\sqrt{\lambda}} \tag{12}$$

is the corresponding standardized random variable, then

$$\lim_{\lambda \to \infty} P\left(a \le \frac{X - \lambda}{\sqrt{\lambda}} \le b \right) = \frac{1}{\sqrt{2\pi}} \int_a^b e^{-u^2/2} \, du \tag{13}$$

i.e., the Poisson distribution approaches the normal distribution as $\lambda \to \infty$ or $(X - \mu)/\sqrt{\lambda}$ is *asymptotically normal*.

Central Limit Theorem

The similarities between the binomial, Poisson, and normal distributions naturally lead us to ask whether there are any other distributions besides the binomial and Poisson that have the normal distribution as the limiting case. The following remarkable theorem reveals that actually a large class of distributions have this property.

Theorem 5-1:   (**Central Limit Theorem**) Let X_1, X_2,..., X_n be independent random variables that are identically distributed (i.e., all have the *same* probability function in the discrete case or density function in the continuous case) and have finite mean μ and variance σ^2. Then if

$$S_n = X_1 + X_2 + \cdots + X_n \quad (n = 1, 2, ...),$$

$$\lim_{n \to \infty} P\left(a \le \frac{S_n - n\mu}{\sigma\sqrt{n}} \le b \right) = \frac{1}{\sqrt{2\pi}} \int_a^b e^{-u^2/2} \, du \qquad (14)$$

that is, the random variable $(S_n - n\mu)/\sigma\sqrt{n}$, which is the standardized variable corresponding to S_n, is asymptotically normal.

The theorem is also true under more general conditions; for example, it holds when X_1, X_2, ..., X_n are independent random variables with the same mean and the same variance but not necessarily identically distributed.

Law of Large Numbers

Theorem 5-2:   (**Law of Large Numbers**) Let x_1, x_2, ..., x_n be mutually independent random variables (discrete or continuous), each having finite mean μ and variance σ^2. Then if $S_n = X_1 + X_2 + \cdots + X_n \quad (n = 1, 2, ...),$

$$\lim_{n\to\infty} P\left(\left|\frac{S_n}{n}\right| - \mu \geq \varepsilon\right) = 0 \qquad (15)$$

Since S_n/n is the arithmetic mean of $X_1 + X_2 + \cdots + X_n$, this theorem states that the probability of the arithmetic mean S_n/n differing from its expected value μ by more than ε approaches zero as $n \to \infty$. A stronger result, which we might expect to be true, is that $\lim_{n\to\infty} S_n / n = \mu$, but that is actually false. However, we can prove that $\lim_{n\to\infty} S_n / n = \mu$ with *probability one*. This result is often called the *strong law of large numbers*, and by contrast, that of Theorem 5-2 is called the *weak law of large numbers*

Chapter 6
SAMPLING THEORY

IN THIS CHAPTER:

✔ *Population and Sample*
✔ *Sampling*
✔ *Random Samples, Random Numbers*
✔ *Population Parameters*
✔ *Sample Statistics*
✔ *Sampling Distributions*
✔ *The Sample Mean*
✔ *Sampling Distribution of Means*
✔ *Sampling Distribution of Proportions*
✔ *Sampling Distribution of Differences and Sums*
✔ *The Sample Variance*
✔ *Frequency Distributions*
✔ *Relative Frequency Distributions*

Population and Sample

Often in practice we are interested in drawing valid conclusions about a large group of individuals or objects. Instead of examining the entire group, called the *population*, which may be difficult or impossible to do, we may examine only a small part of this population, which is called a *sample*. We do this with the aim of inferring certain facts about the population from results found in a sample, a process known as *statistical inference*. The process of obtaining samples is called *sampling*.

Example 6.1. We may wish to draw conclusions about the percentage of defective bolts produced in a factory during a given 6-day week by examining 20 bolts each day produced at various times during the day. In this case all bolts produced during the week comprise the population, while the 120 selected bolts constitute a sample.

Several things should be noted. First, the word *population* does not necessarily have the same meaning as in everyday language, such as "the population of Shreveport is 180,000." Second, the word *population* is often used to denote the observations or measurements rather than individuals or objects. Third, the population can be finite or infinite, with the number being called the *population size*, usually denoted by N. Similarly, the number in the sample is called the *sample size*, denoted by n, and is generally finite.

Sampling

If we draw an object from an urn, we have the choice of replacing or not replacing the object into the urn before we draw again. In the first case a particular object can come up again and again, whereas in the second it can come up only once. Sampling where each member of a population may be chosen more than once is called *sampling with replacement*, while sampling where each member cannot be chosen more than once is called *sampling without replacement*.

You Need to Know

A finite population that is sampled with replacement can theoretically be considered infinite since samples of any size can be drawn without exhausting the population. For most practical purposes, sampling from a finite population that is very large can be considered as sampling from an infinite population.

Random Samples, Random Numbers

Clearly, the reliability of conclusions drawn concerning a population depends on whether the sample is properly chosen so as to represent the population sufficiently well, and one of the important problems of statistical inference is just how to choose a sample.

One way to do this for finite populations is to make sure that each member of the population has the same chance of being in the sample, which is often called a *random sample*. Random sampling can be accomplished for relatively small populations by drawing lots, or equivalently, by using a table of *random numbers* (Appendix G) specially constructed for such purposes.

Because inference from sample to population cannot be certain, we must use the language of probability in any statement of conclusions.

Population Parameters

A population is considered to be known when we know the probability distribution $f(x)$ (probability function or density function) of the associated random variable X. For instance, in Example 6.1, if X is a random variable whose values are the number of defective bolts found during a given 6-day week, then X has probability distribution $f(x)$.

If, for example, X is normally distributed, we say that the population is *normally distributed* or that we have a *normal population.* Similarly, if X is binomially distributed, we say that the population is *binomially distributed* or that we have a *binomial population.*

There will be certain quantities that appear in $f(x)$, such as μ and σ in the case of the normal distribution or p in the case of the binomial distribution. Other quantities such as the median, mode, and skewness can then be determined in terms of these. All such quantities are often called *population parameters.*

Remember

When we are given the population so that we know $f(x)$, then the population parameters are also known.

An important problem that arises when the probability distribution $f(x)$ of the population is not known precisely, although we may have some idea of, or at least be able to make some hypothesis concerning, is the general behavior of $f(x)$. For example, we may have some reason to suppose that a particular population is normally distributed. In that case we may not know one or both of the values μ and σ and so we might wish to draw statistical inferences about them.

Sample Statistics

We can take random samples from the population and then use these samples to obtain values that serve to estimate and test hypothesis about the population parameters.

By way of illustration, let us consider an example where we wish to draw conclusions about the heights of 12,000 adult students by examining only 100 students selected from the population. In this case, X can be a random variable whose values are the various heights. To obtain a sample of size 100, we must first choose one individual at random from the population. This individual can have any one value, say x_1, of the various possible heights, and we can call x_1 the value of a random variable X_1, where the subscript 1 is used since it corresponds to the first individual chosen. Similarly, we choose the second individual for the sample, who can have any one of the values x_2 of the possible heights, and x_2 can be taken as the value of a random variable X_2. We can continue this process up to X_{100} since the sample is size 100. For simplicity let us assume that the sampling is with replacement so that the same individual could conceivably be chosen more than once. In this case, since the sample size is much smaller than the population size, sampling without replacement would give practically the same results as sampling with replacement.

In the general case a sample of size n would be described by the values $x_1, x_2, ..., x_n$ of the random variables $X_1, X_2, ..., X_n$. In this case of sampling with replacement, $X_1, X_2, ..., X_n$ would be independent, identically distributed random variables having probability function $f(x)$. Their joint distribution would then be

$$P(X_1 = x_1, X_2 = x_2,..., X_n = x_n) = f(x_1)f(x_2)\cdots f(x_n)$$

Any quantity obtained from a sample for the purpose of estimating a population parameter is called a *sample statistic*. Mathematically, a sample statistic for a sample of size n can be defined as a function of the random variables $X_1, X_2, ..., X_n$, i.e. $g(X_1,...,X_n)$. The function $g(X_1,...,X_n)$ is another random variable, whose values can be represented by $g(x_1,...,x_n)$.

Note!

The word *statistic* is often used for the random variables or for its values, the particular sense being clear from the context.

In general, corresponding to each population parameter there will be a statistic computed from the sample. Usually the method for obtaining this statistic from the sample is similar to that for obtaining the parameter from a finite population, since a sample consists of a finite set of values. As we shall see, however, this may not always produce the "best estimate," and one of the important problems of sampling theory is to decide how to form the proper sample statistic that will be estimate a given population parameter. Such problems are considered later.

Where possible we shall use Greek letters, such as μ or σ for values of population parameters, and Roman letters, m, s, etc., for values corresponding to sample statistics.

Sampling Distributions

As we have seen, a sample statistic that is computed from $X_1,..., X_n$ is a function of these random variables and is therefore itself a random variable. The probability distribution of a sample statistic is often called the *sampling distribution* of the statistic.

Alternatively, we can consider all possible sample of size n that can be drawn from the population, and for each sample we compute the statistic. In this manner we obtain the distribution of the statistic, which is its sampling distribution.

For a sampling distribution, we can of course compute a mean, variance, standard deviation, etc. The standard deviation is sometimes also called the *standard error*.

The Sample Mean

Let $X_1, X_2,..., X_n$ denote the independent, identically distributed, random variables for a random sample of size n as described above. Then the *mean of the sample* or *sample mean* is a random variable defined by

$$\overline{X} = \frac{X_1 + X_2 + \cdots X_n}{n} \qquad (1)$$

If $x_1, x_2,..., x_n$ denote the values obtained in a particular sample of size n, then the mean for that sample is denoted by

$$\overline{x} = \frac{x_1 + x_2 + \cdots x_n}{n} \qquad (2)$$

Sampling Distribution of Means

Let $f(x)$ be the probability distribution of some given population from which we draw a sample of size n. Then it is natural to look for the probability distribution of the sample statistics $\overline{X}$, which is called the *sampling distribution for the sample mean*, or the *sampling distribution of mean*. The following theorems are important in this connection.

Theorem 6-1: The mean of the sampling distribution of means, denoted by $\mu_{\overline{X}}$, is given by

$$E(\overline{X}) = \mu_{\overline{X}} = \mu \qquad (3)$$

where μ is the mean of the population.

Theorem 6-1 states that the expected value of the sample mean is the population mean.

Theorem 6-2:   If a population is infinite and the sampling is random or if the population is finite and sampling is with replacement, then the variance of the sampling distribution of means, denoted by $\sigma_{\overline{X}}^2$, is given by

$$E\left[\left(\overline{X}-\mu\right)^2\right]=\sigma_{\overline{X}}^2=\frac{\sigma^2}{n} \qquad (4)$$

where σ^2 is the variance of the population.

Theorem 6-3:   If the population is of size N, if sampling is without replacement, and if the sample size is $n \le N$, then the previous equation is replaced by

$$\sigma_{\overline{X}}^2=\frac{\sigma^2}{n}\left(\frac{N-n}{N-1}\right) \qquad (5)$$

while $\mu_{\overline{X}}$ is from Theorem 6-1.

Note that Theorem 6-3 is basically the same as 6-2 as $N \to \infty$.

Theorem 6-4:   If the population from which samples are taken is normally distributed with mean μ and variance σ^2, then the sample mean is normally distributed with mean μ and variance σ^2/n.

Theorem 6-5:   Suppose that the population from which samples are taken has a probability distribution with mean μ and variance σ^2, that is not necessarily a normal distribution. Then the standardized variable associated with $\overline{X}$, given by

$$Z=\frac{\overline{X}-\mu}{\sigma/\sqrt{n}} \qquad (6)$$

is *asymptotically normal*, i.e.,

$$\lim_{n \to \infty} P(Z \le z) = \frac{1}{\sqrt{2\pi}} \int_{-\infty}^{z} e^{-u^2/2} \, du \qquad (7)$$

Theorem 6-5 is a consequence of the central limit theorem. It is assumed here that the population is infinite or that sampling is with replacement. Otherwise, the above is correct if we replace $\sigma / \sqrt{n}$ in Theorem 6-5 by $\sigma_{\bar{X}}^2$ as given in Theorem 6-3.

Example 6.2.   Five hundred ball bearings have a mean weight of 5.02 oz and a standard deviation of 0.30 oz. Find the probability that a random sample of 100 ball bearings chosen from this group will have a combined weight of more than 510 oz.

For the sampling distribution of means, $\mu_{\bar{X}} = \mu = 5.02$ oz, and

$$\sigma_{\bar{X}} = \frac{\sigma}{\sqrt{n}} \sqrt{\frac{N-n}{N-1}} = \frac{0.30}{\sqrt{100}} \sqrt{\frac{500-100}{500-1}} = 0.027 \,.$$

The combined weight will exceed 510 oz if the mean weight of the 100 bearings exceeds 5.10 oz.

$$5.10 \text{ in standard units} = \frac{5.10 - 5.02}{0.027} = 2.96$$

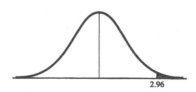

2.96

Figure 6-1

Required Probability = (area to the right of $z = 2.96$)

= (area to the right of $z = 0$) –

(area between $z = 0$ and $z = 2.96$)

= $0.5 - 0.4985 = 0.0015$

Therefore, there are only 3 chances in 2000 of picking a sample of 100 ball bearings with a combined weight exceeding 510 oz.

Sampling Distribution of Proportions

Suppose that a population is infinite and binomially distributed, with p and $q = 1 - p$ being the respective probabilities that any given member exhibits or does not exhibit of a certain property. For example, the population may be all possible tosses of a fair coin, in which the probability of the event heads is $p = \frac{1}{2}$.

Consider all possible samples of size n drawn from this population, and for each sample determine the statistic that is the proportion P of successes. In the case of the coin, P would be the proportion of heads turning up in n tosses. Then we obtain a *sampling distribution* whose mean μ_p and standard deviation σ_p are given by

$$\mu_P = p \qquad \sigma_P = \sqrt{\frac{pq}{n}} = \sqrt{\frac{p(1-p)}{n}} \qquad (8)$$

which can be obtained using Theorem 5-1 and Theorem 5-2, respectively, by placing $\mu = p$, $\sigma = \sqrt{pq}$.

For large values of n ($n \geq 30$), the sampling distribution is very nearly a normal distribution, as is seen from Theorem 6-5.

For finite populations in which sampling is without replacement, the equation for σ_P given above, is replaced by $\sigma_{\bar{X}}$ as given by Theorem 6-3 with $\sigma = \sqrt{pq}$.

Note that the equations for μ_P and σ_P are obtained most easily on dividing by n the mean and standard deviation (np and $\sqrt{npq}$) of the binomial distribution.

Sampling Distribution of Differences and Sums

Suppose that we are given two populations. For each sample of size n_1 drawn from the first population, let us compute a statistic S_1. This yields a sampling distribution for S_1 whose mean and standard deviation we denote by μ_{S_1} and σ_{S_1} , respectively. Similarly for each sample of size n_2 drawn from the second population, let us compute a statistic S_2 whose mean and standard deviation are μ_{S_1} and σ_{S_1} , respectively.

Taking all possible combinations of these samples from the two populations, we can obtain a distribution of the differences, $S_1 - S_2$, which is called the *sampling distribution of differences* of the statistics. The mean and standard deviation of this sampling distribution, denoted respectively by $\mu_{S_1-S_2}$ and $\sigma_{S_1-S_2}$, are given by

$$\mu_{S_1-S_2} = \mu_{S_1} - \mu_{S_2} \qquad \sigma_{S_1-S_2} = \sqrt{\sigma_{S_1}^2 + \sigma_{S_2}^2} \qquad (9)$$

provided that the samples chosen do not in any way depend on each other, i.e., the samples are *independent* (in other words, the random variables S_1 and S_2 are independent).

If, for example, S_1 and S_2 are the sample means from two populations, denoted by $\overline{X}_1, \overline{X}_2$, respectively, then the sampling distribution of the differences of means is given for infinite populations with mean and standard deviation μ_1, σ_1 and μ_2, σ_2, respectively, by

$$\mu_{\overline{X}_1 - \overline{X}_2} = \mu_{\overline{X}_1} - \mu_{\overline{X}_2} = \mu_1 - \mu_2 \qquad (10)$$

and

$$\sigma_{\overline{X}_1 - \overline{X}_2} = \sqrt{\sigma_{\overline{X}_1}^2 + \sigma_{\overline{X}_{12}}^2} = \sqrt{\frac{\sigma_1^2}{n_1} + \frac{\sigma_2^2}{n_2}} \qquad (11)$$

using Theorems 6-1 and 6-2. This result also holds for finite populations if sampling is done with replacement. The standardized variable

$$Z = \frac{\left(\overline{X}_1 - \overline{X}_2\right) - \left(\mu_1 - \mu_2\right)}{\sqrt{\frac{\sigma_1^2}{n_1} + \frac{\sigma_2^2}{n_2}}} \qquad (12)$$

in that case is very nearly normally distributed if n_1 and n_2 are large ($n_1, n_2 \geq 30$). Similar results can be obtained for infinite populations in which sampling is without replacement by using Theorems 6-1 and 6-3.

Corresponding results can be obtained for sampling distributions of differences of proportions from two binomially distributed populations with parameters p_1, q_1 and p_2, q_2, respectively. In this case, S_1 and S_2 correspond to the proportion of successes P_1 and P_2, whose mean and standard deviation of their difference is given by

$$\mu_{P_1 - P_2} = \mu_{P_1} - \mu_{P_2} = p_1 - p_2 \qquad (13)$$

and

$$\sigma_{P_1 - P_2} = \sqrt{\sigma_{P_1}^2 + \sigma_{P_2}^2} = \sqrt{\frac{p_1 q_1}{n_1} + \frac{p_2 q_2}{n_2}} \qquad (14)$$

Instead of taking differences of statistics, we sometimes are interested in the sum of statistics. In that case, the *sampling distribution of the sum of statistics* S_1 and S_2 has mean and standard deviation given by

$$\mu_{S_1+S_2} = \mu_{S_1} + \mu_{S_2} \qquad \sigma_{S_1+S_2} = \sqrt{\sigma^2_{S_1} + \sigma^2_{S_2}} \tag{15}$$

assuming the samples are independent. Results similar to $\mu_{\overline{X}_1-\overline{X}_2}$ and $\sigma_{\overline{X}_1-\overline{X}_2}$ can then be obtained.

Example 6.3.   It has been found that 2% of the tools produced by a certain machine are defective. What is the probability that in a shipment of 400 such tools, 3% or more will prove defective?

$$\mu_P = p = 0.02 \quad \text{and} \quad \sigma_P = \sqrt{\frac{pq}{n}} = \sqrt{\frac{0.02(0.98)}{400}} = \frac{0.14}{20} = 0.007$$

Using the correction for discrete variables, $1/(2n) = 1/800 = 0.00125$, we have $(0.03 - 0.00125)$ in standard units $=$

$$\frac{0.03 - 0.00125 - 0.02}{0.007} = 1.25$$

Required probability   =   (area under normal curve to right of
                                        $z = 1.25$)

                         =   0.1056

If we had not used the correction, we would have obtained 0.0764.

The Sample Variance

If $X_1, X_2, ..., X_n$ denote the random variables for a sample of size n, then the random variable giving the *variance of the sample* or the *sample variance* is defined by

$$S^2 = \frac{\left(X_1 - \overline{X}\right)^2 + \left(X_2 - \overline{X}\right)^2 + \cdots + \left(X_n - \overline{X}\right)^2}{n} \tag{16}$$

Now in Theorem 6-1 we found that $E(\overline{X}) = \mu$, and it would be nice if we could also have $E(S^2) = \sigma^2$. Whenever the expected value of a statistic is equal to the corresponding population parameter, we call the statistic an *unbiased estimator*, and the value an *unbiased estimate*, of this parameter. It turns out, however, that

$$E(S^2) = \mu_{S^2} = \frac{n-1}{n}\sigma^2 \tag{17}$$

which is very nearly σ^2 only for large values of n (say, $n \geq 30$). The desired unbiased estimator is defined by

$$\hat{S}^2 = \frac{n}{n-1}S^2 = \frac{\left(X_1 - \overline{X}\right)^2 + \left(X_2 - \overline{X}\right)^2 + \cdots + \left(X_n - \overline{X}\right)^2}{n-1} \tag{18}$$

so that

$$E(\hat{S}^2) = \sigma^2 \tag{19}$$

Because of this, some statisticians choose to define the sample variance by $\hat{S}^2$ rather than S^2 and they simply replace n by $n - 1$ in the denominator of the definition of S^2 because by doing this, many later results are simplified.

Frequency Distributions

If a sample (or even a population) is large, it is difficult to observe the various characteristics or to compute statistics such as mean or standard deviation. For this reason it is useful to organize or group the *raw data*. As an illustration, suppose that a sample consists of the heights of 100 male students at XYZ University. We arrange the data into *classes* or *categories* and determine the number of individuals belonging to each class, called the *class frequency*. The resulting arrangement, Table 6-1, is called a *frequency distribution* or *frequency table*.

Table 6-1 Heights of 100 Male Students at XYZ University

Height (inches)	Number of Students
60–62	5
63–65	18
66–68	42
69–71	27
72–74	8
TOTAL	100

The first class or category, for example, consists of heights from 60 to 62 inches, indicated by 60–62, which is called *class interval*. Since 5 students have heights belonging to this class, the corresponding class frequency is 5. Since a height that is recorded as 60 inches is actually between 59.5 and 60.5 inches while one recorded as 62 inches is actually between 61.5 and 62.5 inches, we could just as well have recorded

the class interval as 59.5 – 62.5. The next
class interval would then be 62.5 – 65.5, etc.
In the class interval 59.5 – 62.5, the numbers 59.5 and 62.5 are often called *class*
boundaries. The width of the jth class inter-
val, denoted by c_j, which is usually the same for all classes (in which
case it is denoted by c), is the difference between the upper and lower
class boundaries. In this case, $c = 62.5 - 59.5 = 3$.

The midpoint of the class interval, which can be taken as representative of the class, is called the *class mark*. In Table 6.1 the class mark
corresponding to the class interval 60–62 is 61.

A graph for the frequency distribution can be supplied by a histogram, as shown in the figure below, or by a *polygon graph* (often
called a *frequency polygon*) connecting the midpoints of the tops in the
histogram. It is of interest that the shape of the graph seems to indicate
that the sample is drawn from a population of heights that is normally
distributed.

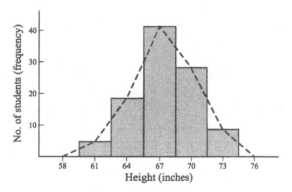

Figure 6-2

Relative Frequency Distributions

If in Table 6.1 we recorded the relative frequency or percentage rather
than the number of students in each class, the result would be a *relative*

or *percentage frequency distribution*. For example, the relative or percentage frequency corresponding to the class 63–65 is 18/100 or 18%. The corresponding histogram is similar to that in Figure 6-1 except that the vertical axis is relative frequency instead of frequency. The sum of the rectangular areas is then 1, or 100%.

We can consider a relative frequency as a probability distribution in which probabilities are replaced by relative frequencies. Since relative frequencies can be thought of as *empirical probabilities*, relative frequency distributions are known as *empirical probability distributions*.

Chapter 7
ESTIMATION THEORY

Unbiased Estimates and Efficient Estimates

As we remarked in Chapter 6, a statistic is called an *unbiased estimator* of a population parameter if the mean or expectation of the statistic is equal to the parameter. The corresponding value of the statistic is then called an *unbiased estimate* of the parameter.

If the sampling distribution of two statistics have the same mean, the statistic with the smaller variance is called a *more efficient estimator* of the mean. The corresponding value of the efficient statistic is then called an *efficient estimate*. Clearly one would in practice prefer to have estimates that are both efficient and unbiased, but this is not always possible.

Point Estimates and Interval Estimates

An estimate of a population parameter given by a single number is called a *point estimate* of the parameter. An estimate of a population parameter given by two numbers between which the parameter may be considered to lie is called an *interval estimate* of the parameter.

Example 7.1.   If we say that a distance is 5.28 feet, we are giving a point estimate. If, on the other hand, we say that the distance is 5.28 ± 0.03 feet, i.e., the distance lies between 5.25 and 5.31 feet, we are giving an interval estimate.

A statement of the error or precision of an estimate is often called its *reliability*.

Confidence Interval Estimates of Population Parameters

Let μ_S and σ_S be the mean and standard deviation (standard error) of the sampling distribution of a statistic S. Then, if the sampling distribution of S is approximately normal (which as we have seen is true for many statistics if the sample size $n \geq 30$), we can expect to find S lying in the interval $\mu_S - \sigma_S$ to $\mu_S + \sigma_S$, $\mu_S - 2\sigma_S$ to $\mu_S + 2\sigma_S$ or $\mu_S - 3\sigma_S$ to $\mu_S + 3\sigma_S$ about 68.27%, 95.45%, and 99.73% of the time, respectively.

Equivalently we can expect to find, or we can be *confident* of finding μ_S in the intervals $S - \sigma_S$ to $S + \sigma_S$, $S - 2\sigma_S$ to $S + 2\sigma_S$, or $S - 3\sigma_S$ to $S + 3\sigma_S$ about 68.27%, 95.45%, and 99.73% of the time, respectively. Because of this, we call these respective intervals the 68.27%, 95.45%, and 99.73% *confidence intervals* for estimating μ_S (i.e., for estimating the population parame-  ter, in this case of an unbiased S). The end numbers of these intervals ($S \pm \sigma_S$, $S \pm 2\sigma_S$, $S \pm 3\sigma_S$) are then called the 68.37%, 95.45%, and 99.73% *confidence limits*.

Similarly, $S \pm 1.96\sigma_S$ and $S \pm 2.58\sigma_S$ are 95% and 99% (or 0.95 and 0.99) confidence limits for μ_S. The percentage confidence is often called the *confidence level*. The numbers 1.96, 2.58, etc., in the confidence limits are called *critical values*, and are denoted by z_C. From confidence levels we can find critical values.

In Table 7.1 we give values of z_C corresponding to various confidence levels used in practice. For confidence levels not presented in the table, the values of z_C can be found from the normal curve area table in Appendix B.

Table 7-1

Confidence Level	99.73%	99%	98%	96%	95.45%
z_C	3.00	2.58	2.33	2.05	2.00

Confidence Level	95%	90%	80%	68.27%	50%
z_C	1.96	1.645	1.28	1.00	0.6745

In cases where a statistic has a sampling distribution that is different from the normal distribution, appropriate modifications to obtain confidence intervals have to be made.

Confidence Intervals for Means

We shall see how to create confidence intervals for the mean of a population using two different cases. The first case shall be when we have a large sample size ($n \geq 30$), and the second case shall be when we have a smaller sample ($n < 30$) and the underlying population is normal.

Large Samples ($n \geq 30$)

If the statistic S is the sample mean $\overline{X}$, then the 95% and 99% confidence limits for estimation of the population mean μ are given by $\overline{X} \pm 1.96\sigma_{\overline{X}}$ and $\overline{X} \pm 2.58\sigma_{\overline{X}}$, respectively. More generally, the confidence limits are given by $\overline{X} \pm z_c \sigma_{\overline{X}}$ where z_c, which depends on the particular level of confidence desired, can be read from Table 7.1. Using the vales of $\sigma_{\overline{X}}$ obtained in Chapter Six, we see that the confidence limits for the population mean are given by

$$\overline{X} \pm z_C \frac{\sigma}{n} \qquad (1)$$

in case sampling from an infinite population or if sampling is done with replacement from a finite population, and by

$$\overline{X} \pm z_C \frac{\sigma}{n} \sqrt{\frac{N-n}{N-1}} \qquad (2)$$

if sampling is done without replacement from a population of finite size N.

In general, the population standard deviation σ is unknown, so that to obtain the above confidence limits, we use the estimator $\hat{S}$ or S.

Example 7.2. Find a 95% confidence interval estimating the mean height of the 1546 male students at XYZ University by taking a sample of size 100. (Assume the mean of the sample, $\overline{x}$, is 67.45 and that the standard deviation of the sample, $\hat{s}$, is 2.93 inches.)

The 95% confidence limits are $\overline{X} \pm 1.96 \dfrac{\sigma}{\sqrt{n}}$.

Using $\overline{x} = 67.45$ inches and $\hat{s} = 2.93$ inches as an estimate of σ, the confidence limits are

$$67.45 \pm 1.96\left(\frac{2.93}{\sqrt{100}} \right) \text{ inches}$$

or

$$67.45 \pm 0.57 \text{ inches}$$

Then the 95% confidence interval for the population mean μ is 66.88 to 68.02 inches, which can be denoted by $66.88 < \mu < 68.02$.

We can therefore say that the probability that the population mean height lies between 66.88 and 68.02 inches is about 95% or 0.95. In symbols, we write $P(66.88 < \mu < 68.02) = 0.95$. This is equivalent to saying that we are 95% *confident* that the population mean (or true mean) lies between 66.88 and 68.02 inches.

Small Samples ($n < 30$) and Population Normal

In this case we use the t distribution (see Chapter Ten) to obtain confidence levels. For example, if $-t_{0.975}$ and $t_{0.975}$ are the values of T for which 2.5% of the area lies in each tail of the t distribution, then a 95% confidence interval for T is given by

$$-t_{0.975} < \frac{(\overline{X} - \mu)\sqrt{n}}{\hat{S}} < t_{0.975} \qquad (3)$$

from which we can see that μ can be estimated to lie in the interval

$$\overline{X} - t_{0.975} \frac{\hat{S}}{\sqrt{n}} < \mu < \overline{X} + t_{0.975} \frac{\hat{S}}{\sqrt{n}} \qquad (4)$$

with 95% confidence. In general the confidence limits for population means are given by

$$\overline{X} \pm t_c \frac{\hat{S}}{\sqrt{n}} \qquad (5)$$

where the t_c values can be read from Appendix C.

A comparison of (5) with (1) shows that for small samples we replace z_c by t_c. For $n > 30$, z_c and t_c are practically equal. It should be noted that an advantage of the small sampling theory (which can of course be used for large samples as well, i.e., it is *exact*) in that $\hat{S}$ appears in (5) so that the sample standard deviation can be used instead of the population standard deviation (which is usually unknown) as in (1).

Sample size is very important! We construct different confidence intervals based on sample size, so make sure you know which procedure to use.

Confidence Intervals for Proportions

Suppose that the statistic S is the proportion of "successes" in a sample of size $n \geq 30$ drawn from a binomial population in which p is the proportion of successes (i.e., the probability of success). Then the confidence limits for p are given by $P \pm z_c \sigma_P$, where P denotes the proportion of success in the sample of size n. Using the values of σ_P obtained in Chapter Six, we see that the confidence limits for the population proportion are given by

$$P \pm z_c \sqrt{\frac{pq}{n}} = P \pm z_c \sqrt{\frac{p(1-p)}{n}} \tag{6}$$

in case sampling from an infinite population or if sampling is with replacement from a finite population. Similarly, the confidence limits are

$$P \pm z_c \sqrt{\frac{pq}{n}} \sqrt{\frac{N-n}{N-1}} \tag{7}$$

if sampling is without replacement from a population of finite size N. Note that these results are obtained from (1) and (2) on replacing $\overline{X}$ by P and σ by $\sqrt{pq}$.

To compute the above confidence limits, we use the sample estimate P for p.

Example 7.3. A sample poll of 100 voters chosen at random from all voters in a given district indicate that 55% of them were in favor of a particular candidate. Find the 99% confidence limits for the proportion of all voters in favor of this candidate.

The 99% confidence limits for the population p are

$$P \pm 1.58\sigma_P = P \pm 2.58\sqrt{\frac{p(1-p)}{n}}$$

$$= 0.55 \pm 2.58\sqrt{\frac{(0.55)(0.45)}{100}}$$

$$= 0.55 \pm 0.13$$

Confidence Intervals for Differences and Sums

If S_1 and S_2 are two sample statistics with approximately normal sampling distributions, confidence limits for the differences of the population parameters corresponding to S_1 and S_2 are given by

$$S_1 - S_2 \pm z_c\sigma_{S_1-S_2} = S_1 - S_2 \pm z_c\sqrt{\sigma_{S_1}^2 + \sigma_{S_2}^2} \qquad (8)$$

while confidence limits for the sum of the population parameters are given by

$$S_1 + S_2 \pm z_c\sigma_{S_1+S_2} = S_1 + S_2 \pm z_c\sqrt{\sigma_{S_1}^2 + \sigma_{S_2}^2} \qquad (9)$$

provided that the samples are independent.

For example, confidence limits for the difference of two population means, in the case where the populations are infinite and have known standard deviations σ_1, σ_2, are given by

$$\overline{X}_1 - \overline{X}_2 \pm z_c\sigma_{\overline{X}_1-\overline{X}_2} = \overline{X}_1 - \overline{X}_2 \pm z_c\sqrt{\frac{\sigma_1^2}{n_1} + \frac{\sigma_2^2}{n_2}} \qquad (10)$$

where $\overline{X}_1$, n_1 and $\overline{X}_2$, n_2 are the respective means and sizes of the two samples drawn from the populations.

Similarly, confidence limits for the difference of two population proportions, where the populations are infinite, are given by

$$P_1 - P_2 \pm z_c \sqrt{\frac{P_1(1-P_1)}{n_1} + \frac{P_2(1-P_2)}{n_2}} \qquad (11)$$

where P_1 and P_2 are the two sample proportions and n_1 and n_2 are the sizes of the two samples drawn from the populations.

Remember

The variance for the difference of means is the same as the variance for the sum of means! In other words,

$$\sigma^2_{X+Y} = \sigma^2_{X-Y}$$

Example 7.4.   In a random sample of 400 adults and 600 teenagers who watched a certain television program, 100 adults and 300 teenagers indicated that they liked it. Construct the 99.73% confidence limits for the difference in proportions of all adults and all teenagers who watched the program and liked it.

Confidence limits for the difference in proportions of the two groups are given by *(11)*, where subscripts 1 and 2 refer to teenagers and adults, respectively, and $Q_1 = 1 - P_1$, $Q_2 = 1 - P_2$. Here $P_1 = 300/600 = 0.50$ and $P_2 = 100/400 = 0.25$ are, respectively, the proportions of teenagers and adults who liked the program. The 99.73% confidence limits are given by

$$0.50 - 0.25 \pm 3\sqrt{\frac{(0.50)(0.50)}{600} + \frac{(0.25)(0.75)}{400}} = 0.25 \pm 0.09 \quad (12)$$

Therefore, we can be 99.73% confident that the true difference in proportions lies between 0.16 and 0.34.

Chapter 8
TEST OF HYPOTHESIS AND SIGNIFICANCE

IN THIS CHAPTER:

✔ *Statistical Decisions*
✔ *Statistical Hypothesis*
✔ *Tests of Hypothesis and Significance*
✔ *Type I and Type II Errors*
✔ *Level of Significance*
✔ *Test Involving the Normal Distribution*
✔ *One-Tailed and Two-Tailed Tests*
✔ *P Value*
✔ *Special Tests*
✔ *Relationship between Estimation Theory and Hypothesis Testing*

Statistical Decisions

Very often in practice we are called upon to make decisions about populations on the basis of sample information. Such decisions are called *statistical decisions.* For example, we may wish to decide on the basis of sample data whether a new serum is really effective in curing a disease, whether one educational procedure is better than another, or whether a given coin is loaded.

Statistical Hypothesis

In attempting to reach decisions, it is useful to make assumptions or guesses about the populations involved. Such assumptions, which may or may not be true, are called *statistical hypotheses* and in general are statements about the probability distributions of the populations.

For example, if we want to decide whether a given coin is loaded, we formulate the hypothesis that the coin is fair, i.e., $p = 0.5$, where p is the probability of heads. Similarly, if we want to decide whether one procedure is better than another, we formulate the hypothesis that there is *no difference* between the two procedures (i.e., any observed differences are merely due to fluctuations in sampling from the *same* population). Such hypotheses are often called *null hypotheses*, denoted by H_0.

Any hypothesis that differs from a given null hypothesis is called an *alternative hypothesis*. For example, if the null hypothesis is $p = 0.5$, possible alternative hypotheses are $p = 0.7$, $p \neq 0.5$, or $p > 0.5$. A hypothesis alternative to the null hypothesis is denoted by H_1.

Tests of Hypothesis and Significance

If on the supposition that a particular hypothesis is true we find that results observed in a random sample differ markedly from those expected under the hypothesis on the basis of pure chance using sampling theory, we would say that the observed differences are *significant* and we would be inclined to reject the hypothesis (or at least not accept it on the basis of the evidence obtained). For example, if 20 tosses of a coin yield 16 heads, we would be inclined to reject the hypothesis that the coin is fair, although it is conceivable that we might be wrong.

You Need to Know

Procedures that enable us to decide whether to accept or reject hypothesis or to determine whether observed samples differ significantly from expected results are called *tests of hypotheses, tests of significance,* or *decision rules.*

Type I and Type II Errors

If we reject a hypothesis when it happens to be true, we say that a *Type I* error has been made. If, on the other hand, we accept a hypothesis when it should be rejected, we say that a *Type II* error has been made. In either case a wrong decision or error in judgment has occurred.

In order for any tests of hypotheses or decision rules to be good, they must be designed so as to minimize errors of decision. This is not a simple matter since, for a given sample size, an attempt to decrease one type of error is accompanied in general by an increase in the other type of error. In practice one type of error may be more serious than the other, and so a compromise should be reached in favor of a limitation of the more serious error. The only way to reduce both types of errors is to increase the sample size, which may or may not be possible.

Level of Significance

In testing a given hypothesis, the maximum probability with which we would be willing to risk a Type I error is called the *level of significance* of the test. This probability is often specified before any samples are drawn so that results obtained will not influence our decision.

In practice a level of significance of 0.05 or 0.01 is customary, although other values are used. If for example a 0.05 or 5% level of significance is chosen in designing a test of a hypothesis, then there are about 5 chances in 100 that we would reject the hypothesis when it should be accepted; i.e., whenever the null hypothesis is true, we are about 95% *confident* that we would make the right decision. In such cases we say that the hypothesis has been *rejected at a* 0.05 *level of significance*, which means that we could be wrong with probability 0.05.

 **Note!**

Choosing your level of significance before you begin testing will greatly aid you in choosing whether to accept or reject a null hypothesis.

Test Involving the Normal Distribution

To illustrate the ideas presented above, suppose that under a given hypothesis, the sampling distribution of a statistic S is a normal distribution with mean μ_S and standard deviation σ_S. The distribution of that standard variable $Z = (S - \mu_S)/\sigma_S$ is the standard normal distribution (mean 0, variance 1) shown in Figure 8-1, and extreme values of Z would lead to the rejection of the hypothesis.

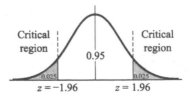

Figure 8-1

As indicated in the figure, we can be 95% confident that, if the hypothesis is true, the z score of an actual sample statistic S will be between -1.96 and 1.96 (since the area under the normal curve between these values is 0.95).

However, if on choosing a single sample at random we find that the z score of its statistic lies *outside* the range -1.96 to 1.96, we would conclude that such an event could happen with the probability of only 0.05 (total shaded area in the figure) if the given hypothesis was true. We would  then say that this z score differed *significantly* from what would be expected under the hypothesis, and we would be inclined to reject the hypothesis.

The total shaded area 0.05 is the level of significance of the test. It represents the probability of our being wrong in rejecting the hypothesis, i.e., the probability of making a Type I error. Therefore, we say that the hypothesis is *rejected at a* 0.05 *level of significance* or that the z score of the given sample statistic is *significant* at a 0.05 *level of significance.*

The set of z scores outside the range -1.96 to 1.96 constitutes what is called the *critical region* or *region of rejection of the hypothesis* or *the region of significance.* The set of z scores inside the range -1.96 to 1.96 could then be called the *region of acceptance of the hypothesis* or the *region of nonsignificance.*

On the basis of the above remarks, we can formulate the following decision rule:

(a) Reject the hypothesis at a 0.05 level of significance if the z score of the statistic S lies outside the range -1.96 to 1.96 (i.e., if either $z > 1.96$ or $z < -1.96$). This is equivalent to saying that the observed sample statistic is significant at the 0.05 level.

(b) Accept the hypothesis (or, if desired, make no decision at all) otherwise.

It should be noted that other levels of significance could have been used. For example, if a 0.01 level were used we would replace 1.96 everywhere above by 2.58 (see Table 8.1). Table 7.1 can also be used since the sum of the level of significance and level of confidence is 100%.

One-Tailed and Two-Tailed Tests

In the above test we displayed interest in extreme values of the statistic S or its corresponding z score on both sides of the mean, i.e., in both tails of the distribution. For this reason such tests are called *two-tailed tests* or *two-sided tests*.

Often, however, we may be interested only in extreme values to one side of the mean, i.e., in one tail of the distribution, as for example, when we are testing the hypothesis that one process is better that another (which is different from testing whether one process is better or worse than the other). Such tests are called *one-tailed tests* or *one-sided tests*. In such cases the critical region is a region to one side of the distribution, with area equal to the level of significance.

Table 8.1, which gives values of z for both one-tailed and two-tailed tests at various levels of significance, will be useful for reference purposes. Critical values of z for other levels of significance are found by use of the table of normal curve areas.

Table 8-1

Level of Significance α	0.10	0.05	0.01	0.005
Critical Values of z for One-Tailed Tests	−1.28 *or* 1.28	−1.645 *or* 1.645	−2.33 *or* 2.33	−2.58 *or* 2.58
Critical Values of z for Two-Tailed Tests	−1.645 *and* 1.645	−1.96 *and* 1.96	−2.58 *and* 2.58	−2.81 *and* 2.81

P Value

In most of the tests we will consider, the null hypothesis H_0 will be an assertion that a population parameter has a specific value, and the alternative hypothesis H_1 will be one of the following two assertions:

    (i) The parameter is greater than the stated value (right-tailed test).

(ii) The parameter is less that the stated value (left-tailed test).
(iii) The parameter is either greater than or less than the stated value (two-tailed test).

In Cases (*i*) and (*ii*), H_1 has a single direction with respect to the parameter, and in case (*iii*), H_1 is bi-directional. After the test has been performed and the test statistic S computed, the P value of the test is the probability that a value of S in the direction(s) of H_1 and as extreme as the one that actually did occur if H_0 were true.

For example, suppose the standard deviation σ of a normal population is known to be 3, and H_0 asserts that the mean μ is equal to 12. A random sample of size 36 drawn from the population yields a sample mean $\bar{x} = 12.95$. The test statistic is chosen to be

$$Z = \frac{\bar{X}-12}{\sigma/\sqrt{n}} = \frac{\bar{X}-12}{0.5},$$

which, if H_0 is true, is the standard normal variable. The test value of Z is the following:

$$Z = \frac{12.95-12}{0.5} = 1.9.$$

The P value for the test then depends on the alternative hypothesis H_1 as follows:

(i) For H_1: $\mu > 12$ [case (*i*) above], the P value is the probability that a random sample of size 36 would yield a sample mean of 12.95 or more if the true mean were 12, i.e., $P(Z \geq 19) = 0.029$. In other words, the chances are about 3 in 100 that $\bar{x} \geq 12.95$ if $\mu = 12$.
(ii) For H_1: $\mu < 12$ [case (*ii*) above], the P value is the probability that a random sample of size 36 would yield a sample mean of

12.95 or less if the true mean were 12, i.e., $P(Z \le 19) = 0.971$. In other words, the chances are about 97 in 100 that $\bar{x} \le 12.95$ if $\mu = 12$.

(iii) For $H_1: \mu \ne 12$ [case (iii) above], the P value is the probability that a random sample mean 0.95 or more units away from 12, i.e., $\bar{x} \ge 12.95$ or $\bar{x} \le 11.05$, if the true mean were 12. Here the P value is $P(Z \ge 19) + P(Z \le -19) = 0.057$, which says the chances are about 6 in 100 that $|\bar{x} - 12| \ge 0.095$ if $\mu = 12$.

Small P values provide evidence for rejecting the null hypothesis in favor of the alternative hypothesis, and large P values provide evidence for not rejecting the null hypothesis in favor of the alternative hypothesis. In case (i) of the above example, the small P value 0.029 is a fairly strong indicator that the population mean is greater than 12, whereas in case (ii), the large P value 0.971 strongly suggests that $H_0 : \mu = 12$ should not be rejected in favor of $H_0 : \mu < 12$. In case (iii), the P value 0.057 provides evidence for rejecting H_0 in favor of $H_0 : \mu \ne 12$ but not as much evidence as is provided for rejecting H_0 in favor of $H_0 : \mu > 12$.

It should be kept in mind that the P value and the level of significance do not provide criteria for rejecting or not rejecting the null hypothesis by itself, but for rejecting or not rejecting the null hypothesis in favor of the alternative hypothesis. As the previous example illustrates, identical test results and different significance levels can lead to different conclusions regarding the same null hypothesis in relation to different alternative hypothesis.

When the test statistic S is the standard normal random variable, the table in Appendix B is sufficient to compute the P value, but when S is one of the t, F, or chi-square random variables, all of which have different distributions depending on their degrees of freedom, either computer software or more extensive tables than those in Appendices C, D, and E will be needed to compute the P value.

Example 8.1. The mean lifetime of a sample of 100 fluorescent light bulbs produced by a company is computed to be 1570 hours with a standard deviation of 120 hours. If μ is the mean lifetime of all the bulbs produced by the company, test the hypothesis $\mu = 1600$ hours against the alternative hypothesis $\mu \neq 1600$ hours. Use a significance level of 0.05 and find the P value of the test,

We must decide between the two hypotheses

$$H_0 : \mu = 1600 \text{ hours} \qquad H_0 : \mu \neq 1600 \text{ hours}$$

A two-tailed test should be used here since $\mu \neq 1600$ includes both values large and smaller than 1600.

For a two-tailed test at a level of significance of 0.05, we have the following decision rule:

1. Reject H_0 if the z score of the sample mean is outside the range -1.96 to 1.96.
2. Accept H_0 (or withhold any decision) otherwise.

The statistic under consideration is the sample mean $\overline{X}$. The sampling distribution of X has a mean $\mu_{\overline{X}} = \mu$ and standard deviation $\sigma_{\overline{X}} = \sigma / \sqrt{n}$, where μ and σ are the mean and standard deviation of the population of all bulbs produced by the company.

Under the hypothesis H_0, we have $\mu = 1600$ and $\sigma_{\overline{X}} = \sigma / \sqrt{n} = 120 / \sqrt{100} = 12$, using the sample standard deviation as an estimate of σ. Since $Z = (\overline{X} - 1600) / 12 = (1570 - 1600) / 12 = -2.50$ lies outside the range -1.96 to 1.96, we reject H_0 at a 0.05 level of significance.

The P value of the two tailed test is $P(Z \leq -2.50) + P(Z \geq 2.50) = 0.0124$, which is the probability that a mean lifetime of less than 1570 hours or more than 1630 hours would occur by chance if H_0 were true.

Special Tests

For large samples, many statistics S have nearly normal distributions with mean μ_S and standard deviation σ_S. In such cases we can use the above results to formulate decision rules or tests of hypotheses and significance. The following special cases are just a few of the statistics of practical interest. In each case the results hold for infinite populations or for sampling with replacement. For sampling without replacement from finite populations, the results must be modified. We shall only consider the cases for large samples ($n \geq 30$).

1. **Means.** Here $S = \overline{X}$, the sample mean; $\mu_S = \mu_{\overline{X}} = \mu$, the population mean; $\sigma_S = \sigma_{\overline{X}} = \sigma / \sqrt{n}$, where σ is the population standard deviation and n is the sample size. The standardized variable is given by

$$Z = \frac{\overline{X} - \mu}{\sigma / \sqrt{n}} \tag{1}$$

When necessary the observed sample standard deviation, s (or $\hat{s}$), is used to estimate σ.

To test the null hypothesis H_0 that the population mean is $\mu = a$, we would use the statistic (1). Then, if the alternative hypothesis is $\mu = a$, using a two-tailed test, we would accept H_0 (or at least not reject it) at the 0.05 level if for a particular sample of size n having mean $\overline{x}$

$$-1.96 \leq \frac{\overline{x} - a}{\sigma / \sqrt{n}} \leq 1.96 \tag{2}$$

and would reject it otherwise. For other significance levels we would change (2) appropriately. To test H_0 against the alternative hypothesis that the population mean is greater than a, we would use a one-tailed test and accept H_0 (or at least not reject it) at the 0.05 level if

$$\frac{\overline{x} - a}{\sigma / \sqrt{n}} < 1.645 \tag{3}$$

(see Table 8.1) and reject it otherwise. To test H_0 against the alternative hypothesis that the population mean is less than a, we would accept H_0 at the 0.05 level if

$$\frac{\bar{x} - a}{\sigma / \sqrt{n}} > 1.645 \tag{4}$$

2. **Proportions**   Here $S = P$, the proportion of "successes" in a sample; $\mu_S = \mu_P = P$, where p is the population proportion of successes and n is the sample size; $\sigma_S = \sigma_P = \sqrt{pq/n}$, where $q = 1 - p$. The standardized variable is given by

$$Z = \frac{P - p}{\sqrt{pq/n}} \tag{5}$$

In case $P = X/n$, where X is the actual number of successes in a sample, (5) becomes

$$Z = \frac{X - np}{\sqrt{npq}} \tag{6}$$

Remarks similar to those made above about one- and two-tailed tests for means can be made.

3. **Differences of Means**   Let $\bar{X}_1$ and $\bar{X}_2$ be the sample means obtained in large samples of sizes n_1 and n_2 drawn from respective populations having means μ_1 and μ_2 and standard deviations σ_1 and σ_2. Consider the null hypothesis that there is *no difference* between the population means, i.e., $\mu_1 = \mu_2$. From our discussion on the sampling distributions of differences and sums (Chapter 6), on placing $\mu_1 = \mu_2$ we see that the sampling distribution of differences in means is approximately normal with mean and standard deviation given by

$$\mu_{\overline{X}_1 - \overline{X}_2} = 0 \qquad \sigma_{\overline{X}_1 - \overline{X}_2} = \sqrt{\frac{\sigma_1^2}{n_1} + \frac{\sigma_2^2}{n_2}} \qquad (7)$$

where we can, if necessary, use the observed sample standard deviations s_1 and s_2 (or $\hat{s}_1$ and $\hat{s}_2$) as estimates of σ_1 and σ_2. By using the standardized variable given by

$$Z = \frac{\overline{X}_1 - \overline{X}_2 - 0}{\sigma_{\overline{X}_1 - \overline{X}_2}} = \frac{\overline{X}_1 - \overline{X}_2}{\sigma_{\overline{X}_1 - \overline{X}_2}} \qquad (8)$$

in a manner similar to that described in Part 1 above, we can test the null hypothesis against an alternative hypothesis (or the significance of an observed difference) at an appropriate level of significance.

4. **Differences of Proportions**   Let P_1 and P_2 be the sample proportions obtained in large samples of sizes n_1 and n_2 drawn from respective populations having proportions p_1 and p_2. Consider the null hypothesis that there is *no difference* between the population proportions, i.e., $p_1 = p_2$, and thus that the samples are really drawn from the same population.

From our discussions about the differences of proportions in Chapter 6, on placing $p_1 = p_2 = p$, we see that the sampling distribution of differences in proportions is approximately normal with mean and standard deviation given by

$$\mu_{P_1 - P_2} = 0 \qquad \sigma_{P_1 - P_2} = \sqrt{p(1-p)\left(\frac{1}{n_1} + \frac{1}{n2}\right)} \qquad (9)$$

where $\overline{P} = \dfrac{n_1 P_1 + n_2 P_2}{n_1 + n_2}$ is used as an estimate of the population proportion p.

By using the standardized variable

$$Z = \frac{P_1 - P_2 - 0}{\sigma_{P_1 - P_2}} = \frac{P_1 - P_2}{\sigma_{P_1 - P_2}} \qquad (10)$$

we can observe differences at an appropriate level of significance and thereby test the null hypothesis.

Tests involving other statistics can similarly be designed.

Relationship between Estimation Theory and Hypothesis Testing

From the above remarks one cannot help but notice that there is a relationship between estimation theory involving confidence intervals and the theory of hypothesis testing. For example, we note that the result (2) for accepting H_0 at the 0.05 level is equivalent to the result (1) in Chapter 7, leading to the 95% confidence interval

$$\overline{x} - \frac{1.96\sigma}{\sqrt{n}} \leq \mu \leq \overline{x} - \frac{1.96\sigma}{\sqrt{n}} \qquad (11)$$

Thus, at least in the case of two-tailed tests, we could actually employ the confidence intervals of Chapter 7 to test the hypothesis. A similar result for one-tailed tests would require one-sided confidence intervals.

Example 8.2. Consider Example 8.1. A 95% confidence interval for Example 8.1 is the following

$$1570 - \frac{(1.96)(120)}{\sqrt{100}} \leq \mu \leq 1570 + \frac{(1.96)(120)}{\sqrt{100}}$$

which is

$$1570 - 23.52 \leq \mu \leq 1570 + 23.52$$

This leads to an interval of (1546.48, 1593.52). Notice that this does not contain the alleged mean of 1600, thus leading us to reject H_0.

Chapter 9
CURVE FITTING, REGRESSION, AND CORRELATION

Curve Fitting

Very often in practice a relationship is found to exist between two (or more) variables, and one wishes to express this relationship in mathematical form by determining an equation connecting the variables.

A first step is the collection of data showing corresponding values of the variables. For example, suppose x and y denote, respectively, the height and weight of an adult male. Then a sample of n individuals would reveal the heights $x_1, x_2, ..., x_n$ and the corresponding weights $y_1, y_2, ..., y_n$.

A next step is to plot the points $(x_1, y_1), (x_2, y_2), ..., (x_n, y_n)$ on a rectangular coordinate system. The resulting set of points is sometimes called a *scatter diagram.*

From the scatter diagram it is often possible to visualize a smooth curve approximating the data. Such a curve is called an *approximating curve.* In Figure 9-1, for example, the data appear to be approximated well by a straight line, and we say that a *linear relationship* exists between the variables. In Figure 9-2, however, although a relationship exists between the variables, it is not a linear relationship and so we call it a *nonlinear relationship.* In Figure 9-3 there appears to be no relationship between the variables.

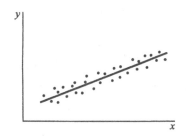

Figure 9-1

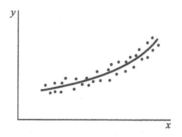

Figure 9-2

Figure 9-3

The general problem of finding equations approximating curves that fit given sets of data is called *curve fitting*. In practice the type of equation is often suggested from the scatter diagram. For Figure 9-1 we could use a straight line:

$$y = a + bx$$

while for Figure 9-2 we could try a *parabola* or *quadratic* curve:

$$y = a + bx + cx^2$$

For the purposes of this book, we will only concern ourselves with the data sets exhibiting a linear relationship.

Sometimes it helps to plot scatter diagrams in terms of *transformed variables*. For example, if log y vs. log x leads to a straight line, we would try log $y = a + bx$ as an equation for the approximating curve.

Regression

One of the main purposes of curve fitting is to estimate one of the variables (the *dependent variable*) from the other (the *independent variable*). The process of estimation is often referred to as a *regression*. If y is to be estimated from x by means of some equation, we call the equation a *regression equation of y on x* and the corresponding curve a *regression curve of y on x*. Since we are only considering the linear case, we can call this the *regression line of y on x*.

The Method of Least Squares

Generally, more than one curve of a given type will appear to fit a set of data. To avoid individual judgment in constructing lines, parabolas, or other approximating curves, it is necessary to agree on a definition of a "best-fitting line," "best-fitting parabola," etc.

To motivate a possible definition, consider Figure 9-4 in which the data points are $(x_1, y_1),...,(x_n, y_n)$. For a given value of x, say x_1, there will be a difference between the value y_1 and the corresponding value as determined by the curve C. We denote the difference by d_1, which is sometimes referred to as a *deviation error*, or *residual* and may be positive, negative, or zero. Similarly, corresponding values $x_2, ..., x_n$, we obtain the deviations $d_2, ..., d_n$.

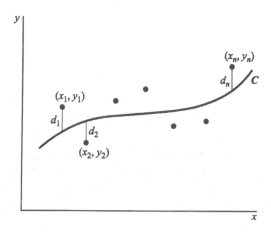

Figure 9-4

A measure of the fit of the curve C to the set of data is provided by the quantity $d_1^2 + d_2^2 + \cdots d_n^2$. If this is small, the fit is good; if it is large, the fit is bad. We therefore make the following definition.

Definition   Of all curves in a given family of curves approximating a set of n data points, a curve having the property that

$$d_1^2 + d_2^2 + \cdots d_n^2 = \text{a minimum}$$

is called a *best-fitting curve* in the family.

A curve having this property is said to fit the data in the *least-squares sense* and is called a *least-squares regression curve*, or simply a *least-squares curve*. A line having this property is called a *least-squares line*; a parabola that has this property is called a *least-squares parabola*; etc.

It is customary to employ the new definition when x is the independent variable and y is the dependent variable. If x is the dependent variable, the definition is modified by considering horizontal deviations instead of vertical deviations, which amounts to interchanging the x and

y axes. These two definitions lead in general to two different least-squares curves. Unless otherwise specified we shall consider y the dependent and x the independent variable

You Need to Know

It is possible to define another least-squares curve by considering perpendicular distances from the data points to the curve instead of either vertical or horizontal distances. However, this is not used very often.

The Least-Squares Line

By using the above definition, we can show that the least-squares line approximating the set of points $(x_1, y_1),...,(x_n, y_n)$ has the equation

$$y = a + bx \qquad (1)$$

where the constants a and b are determined by solving simultaneously the equations

$$\sum y = an + b \sum x$$
$$\sum xy = a \sum x + b \sum x^2 \qquad (2)$$

which are called the *normal equations* for the least-squares line. Note that we have for brevity used $\sum y$, $\sum xy$ instead of $\sum_{j=1}^{n} y_j$, $\sum_{j=1}^{n} x_j y_j$.

The normal equation (2) is easily remembered by observing that the first equation can be obtained formally by summing on both sides of (1), while the second equation is obtained formally by first multiplying both sides of (1) by x and then summing. Of course, this is not a derivation of the normal equations but only a means for remembering them.

The values of a and b obtained from (2) are given by

$$a = \frac{\left(\sum y\right)\left(\sum x^2\right) - \left(\sum x\right)\left(\sum xy\right)}{n \sum x^2 - \left(\sum x\right)^2} \qquad b = \frac{n \sum xy - \left(\sum x\right)\left(\sum y\right)}{n \sum x^2 - \left(\sum x\right)^2} \quad (3)$$

The result for b can also be written as

$$b = \frac{\sum (x - \bar{x})(y - \bar{y})}{\sum (x - \bar{x})^2} \quad (4)$$

Here, as usual, a bar indicates *mean*, e.g. $\bar{x} = \left(\sum x\right)/n$. Division of both sides of the first normal equation in (2) by n yields

$$\bar{y} = a + b\bar{x} \quad (5)$$

If desired, we can first find b from (3) or (4) and then use (5) to find $a = \bar{y} - b\bar{x}$. This is equivalent to writing the least-squares line as

$$y - \bar{y} = b(x - \bar{x}) \quad \text{or} \quad y - \bar{y} = \frac{\sum (x - \bar{x})(y - \bar{y})}{\sum (x - \bar{x})^2}(x - \bar{x}) \quad (6)$$

The result (6) shows that the constant b, which is the *slope* of the line (1), is the fundamental constant in determining the line. From (6) it is also seen that the least-squares line passes through the point $(\bar{x}, \bar{y})$, which is called the *centroid* or *center of gravity* of the data.

The slope b of the regression line is independent of the origin of the coordinates. This means that if we make the transformation (often called a *translation of axes*) given by

$$x = x' + h \qquad y = y' + k \qquad (7)$$

where h and k are any constants, then b is also given by

$$b = \frac{n\sum x'y' - \left(\sum x'\right)\left(\sum y'\right)}{n\sum x'^2 - \left(\sum x'\right)^2} = \frac{\sum (x - \bar{x}')(y - \bar{y}')}{\sum \left(x' - \bar{x}'\right)^2} \qquad (8)$$

where x, y have simply been replaced by x', y' [for this reason we say that b is *invariant under the transformation* (7)]. It should be noted, however, that a, which determines the intercept on the x axis, does depend on the origin (and so is not invariant).

In the particular case where $h = \bar{x}, k = \bar{y}$, (8) simplifies to

$$b = \frac{\sum x'y'}{\sum x'^2} \qquad (9)$$

The results (8) and (9) are often useful in simplifying the labor involved in obtaining the least-squares line.

The above remarks also hold for the regression line of x on y. The results are formally obtained by simply interchanging x and y. For example, the least-squares regression line of x on y is

$$x - \bar{x} = \frac{\sum (x - \bar{x})(y - \bar{y})}{\sum (y - \bar{y})^2}(y - \bar{y}) \qquad (10)$$

It should be noted that in general (10) is not the same as (6).

Remember

You should try to find the equation for the regression line if and only if your data set has a linear relationship.

Example 9.1. Table 9-1 shows the respective heights x and y of a sample of 12 fathers and their oldest sons. Find the least-squares regression line of y on x.

Table 9-1

Height x of Father (inches)	65	63	67	64	68	62
Height y of Son (inches)	68	66	68	65	69	66

Height x of Father (inches)	70	66	68	67	69	71
Height y of Son (inches)	68	65	71	67	68	70

The regression line of y on x is given by $y = ax + b$ are obtained by solving the normal equations

$$\sum y = an + b\sum x \quad \text{and} \quad \sum xy = a\sum x + b\sum x^2$$

The sums are computed as follows:

Table 9-2

x	y	x^2	xy	y^2
65	68	4225	4420	4624
63	66	3969	4158	4356
67	68	4489	4556	4624
64	65	4096	4160	4225
68	69	4624	4692	4761
62	66	3844	4092	4356
70	68	4900	4760	4624
66	65	4356	4290	4225
68	71	4624	4828	5041
67	67	4489	4489	4489
69	68	4761	4692	4624
71	70	5041	4970	4900
$\sum x = 800$	$\sum y = 811$	$\sum x^2 = 53{,}418$	$\sum xy = 54{,}107$	$\sum y^2 = 54{,}849$

Using these sums, the normal equations become

$12a + 800b$	$=$	811
$800a + 53{,}418b$	$=$	$54{,}107$

For which we find $a = 35.82$ and $b = 0.476$, so that $y = 35.82 + 0.476x$ is the equation for the regression line.

The Least-Squares Regression Line in Terms of Sample Variances and Covariance

The sample variances and covariance of x and y are given by

$$s_x^2 = \frac{\sum (x - \bar{x})^2}{n}, \quad s_y^2 = \frac{(y - \bar{y})^2}{n}, \quad s_{xy} = \frac{\sum (x - \bar{x})(y - \bar{y})}{n} \quad (11)$$

In terms of these, the least-squares regression lines of y on x and x on y can be written, respectively, as

$$y - \bar{y} = \frac{s_{xy}}{s_x^2}(x - \bar{x}) \quad \text{and} \quad x - \bar{x} = \frac{s_{xy}}{s_y^2}(y - \bar{y}) \qquad (12)$$

if we formally define the *sample correlation coefficient* by

$$r = \frac{s_{xy}}{s_x s_y} \qquad (13)$$

then (12) can be written

$$\frac{y - \bar{y}}{s_y} = r\frac{(x - \bar{x})}{s_x} \quad \text{and} \quad \frac{x - \bar{x}}{s_x} = r\frac{(y - \bar{y})}{s_y} \qquad (14)$$

In view of the fact that $(x - \bar{x})/s_x$ and $(y - \bar{y})/s_y$ are standardized sample values or standard scores, the results in (14) provide a simple way of remembering the regression lines. It is clear that the two lines in (14) are different unless $r = \pm 1$, in which case all sample points lie in a line and there is *perfect linear correlation and regression.*

It is also of interest to note that if the two regression lines (14) are written as $y = ax + b$, $x = c + dy$, respectively, then

$$bd = r^2 \qquad (15)$$

Up to now we have not considered the precise significance of the correlation coefficient but have only defined it formally in terms of the variances and covariance.

Standard Error of Estimate

If we let y_{est} denote the estimated value of y for a given value of x, as obtained from the regression curve of y on x, then a measure of the scatter about the regression curve is supplied by the quantity

$$S_{y,x} = \sqrt{\frac{\sum(y - y_{est})^2}{n}} \tag{16}$$

which is called the *standard error of estimate* y on x. Since $\sum(y - y_{est})^2 = \sum d^2$, as used in the definition we saw earlier, we see that out of all possible regression curves the least-squares curve has the smallest standard error of estimate.

In the case of a regression line $y_{est} = a + bx$, with a and b given by (2), we have

$$s_{y,x}^2 = \frac{\sum y^2 - a\sum y - b\sum xy}{n} \tag{17}$$

or

$$s_{y-x}^2 = \frac{\sum(y - \bar{y})^2 - b\sum(x - \bar{x})(y - \bar{y})}{n} \tag{18}$$

We can also express $s_{y,x}^2$ for the least-squares regression line in terms of variance and correlation coefficient as

$$s_{y,x}^2 = s_y^2(1 - r^2) \tag{19}$$

from which it incidentally follows as a corollary that $r^2 \leq 1$, i.e., $-1 \leq r \leq 1$.

The standard error of estimate has properties analogous to those of standard deviation. For example, if we construct pairs of lines parallel to the regression line of y on x at respective vertical distances $s_{y,x}$, and $2s_{y,x}$, and $3s_{y,x}$ from it, we should find if n is large enough that there would be included between these pairs of lines about 68%, 95%, and 99.7% of the sample points, respectively.

Just as there is an unbiased estimate of population variance given by $\hat{s}^2 = ns^2/(n-1)$, so there is an unbiased estimate of the square of the standard error of estimate. This is given by $\hat{s}^2_{y,x} = n\hat{s}^2_{y,x}/(n-2)$. For this reason some statisticians prefer to give (16) with $n-2$ instead of n in the denominator.

The above remarks are easily modified for the regression line of x on y (in which case the standard error of estimate is denoted by $s_{x,y}$) or for nonlinear or multiple regression.

The Linear Correlation Coefficient

Up to now we have defined the correlation coefficient formally by (13) but have not examined its significance. In attempting to do this, let us note that from (19) and the definitions of $s_{y,x}$ and s_y, we have

$$r^2 = 1 - \frac{\sum(y - y_{est})^2}{\sum(y - \bar{y})^2} \tag{20}$$

Now we can show that

$$\sum(y - \bar{y})^2 = \sum(y - y_{est})^2 + \sum(y_{est} - \bar{y})^2 \tag{21}$$

The quantity on the left of (*21*) is called the *total variation*. The first sum on the right of (*21*) is then called the *unexplained variation*, while the second sum is called the *explained variation*. This terminology arises because the deviations $y - y_{est}$ behave in a random or unpredictable manner while the deviations $y_{est} - \bar{y}$ are explained by the least-squares regression line and so tend to follow a definite pattern. It follows from (*20*) and (*21*) that

$$r^2 = \frac{\sum (y_{est} - \bar{y})^2}{\sum (y - \bar{y})^2} = \quad \frac{\text{explained variation}}{\text{total variation}} \quad (22)$$

Therefore, r^2 can be interpreted as the fraction of the total variation that is explained by the least-squares regression line. In other words, r measures *how well* the least-squares regression line fits the sample data. If the total variation is *all* explained by the regression line, i.e., $r^2 = 1$ or $r = \pm 1$, we say that there is a *perfect linear correlation* (and in such case also *perfect linear regression*). On the  other hand, if the total variation is all unexplained, then the explained variation is zero and so $r = 0$. In practice the quantity r^2, sometimes call the *coefficient of determination*, lies between 0 and 1.

The correlation coefficient can be computed from either of the results

$$r = \frac{s_{xy}}{s_x s_y} = \frac{\sum (x - \bar{x})(y - \bar{y})}{\sqrt{\sum (x - \bar{x})^2} \sqrt{\sum (y - \bar{y})^2}} \quad (23)$$

or

$$r^2 = \frac{\sum (y_{est} - \bar{y})^2}{\sum (y - \bar{y})^2} = \quad \frac{\text{explained variation}}{\text{total variation}} \quad (24)$$

which for linear regression are equivalent. The formula (23) is often referred to as the *product-moment formula* for linear regression.

Formulas equivalent to those above, which are often used in practice, are

$$r = \frac{n\sum xy - \left(\sum x\right)\left(\sum y\right)}{\sqrt{[n\sum x^2 - \left(\sum x\right)^2][n\sum y^2 - \left(\sum y\right)^2]}} \qquad (25)$$

and

$$r = \frac{\overline{xy} - \overline{x}\,\overline{y}}{\sqrt{(\overline{x^2} - \overline{x}^2)(\overline{y^2} - \overline{y}^2)}} \qquad (26)$$

If we use the transformation on (7), we find

$$r = \frac{n\sum x'y' - \left(\sum x'\right)\left(\sum y'\right)}{\sqrt{[n\sum x'^2 - \left(\sum x'\right)^2][n\sum y'^2 - \left(\sum y'\right)^2]}} \qquad (27)$$

which shows that r is invariant under a translation of axes. In particular, if $h = \overline{x}$, $k = \overline{y}$, (27) becomes

$$r = \frac{\sum x'y'}{\sqrt{\left(\sum x'^2\right)\left(\sum y'^2\right)}} \qquad (28)$$

which is often useful in computation.

The linear correlation coefficient may be positive or negative. If r is positive, y tends to *increase* with x (the slope of the least-squares regression line is positive) while if r is negative, y tends to *decrease* with x (the slope is negative). The sign is *automatically* taken into account if we use the result (23), (25), (26), (27), or (28). However, if we use (24) to obtain r, we must apply the proper sign.

Generalized Correlation Coefficient

The definition (23) [or any equivalent forms (25) through (28)] for the correlation coefficient involves only sample values x, y. Consequently, it yields the same number for all forms of regression curves and is useless as a measure of fit, except in the case of linear regression, where it happens to coincide with (24). However, the latter definition, i.e.,

$$r^2 = \frac{\sum(y_{est} - \bar{y})^2}{\sum(y - \bar{y})^2} \qquad \frac{\text{explained variation}}{\text{total variation}} \qquad (29)$$

does reflect the form of the regression curve (via the y_{est}) and so is suitable as the definition of a *generalized correlation coefficient r*. We use (29) to obtain nonlinear correlation coefficients (which measure how well a *nonlinear regression curve* fits the data) or, by appropriate generalization, *multiple correlation coefficients*. The connection (19) between the correlation coefficient and the standard error of estimate holds as well for nonlinear correlation.

Example 9.2.   Find the coefficient of determination and the coefficient of correlation from Example 8.2.

Recall that the correlation of determination is r^2 :

$$r^2 = \quad \begin{array}{l}\text{explained variation=}\\ \text{total variation}\end{array} \quad \frac{19.22}{38.92} = 0.4938$$

The coefficient of correlation is simply r.

$$r^2 = \pm\sqrt{0.4938} = \pm0.7027$$

Since the variable y_{est} increases as x increases (i.e., the slope of the regression line is positive), the correlation is positive, and we therefore write $r = 0.7027$, or $r = 0.70$ to two significant figures.

Since a correlation coefficient merely measures how well a given regression curve (or surface) fits sample data, it is clearly senseless to use a linear correlation coefficient where the data is nonlinear. Suppose, however, that one does apply (23) to nonlinear data and obtains a value that is numerically considerably less than 1. Then the conclusion to be drawn is not that there is *little correlation* (a conclusion sometimes reached by those unfamiliar with the fundamentals of correlation theory) but that there is *little linear* correlation. There may be in fact a *large* nonlinear correlation.

Correlation and Dependence

Whenever two random variables X and Y have a nonzero correlation coefficient, r, we know that they are *dependent* in the probability sense. Furthermore, we can use an equation of the form (6) to *predict* the value of Y from the value of X.

You Need to Know ✓

It is important to realize that "correlation" and "dependence" in the above sense do not necessarily imply a direct causation interdependence of X and Y.

Example 9.3. If X represents teachers' salaries over the years while Y represents the amount of crime, the correlation coefficient may be different from zero and we may be able to find a regression line predicting one variable from the other. But we would hardly be willing to say that there is a direct interdependence between X and Y.

Chapter 10
OTHER PROBABILITY DISTRIBUTIONS

IN THIS CHAPTER:

✔ *The Multinomial Distribution*
✔ *The Hypergeometric Distribution*
✔ *The Uniform Distribution*
✔ *The Cauchy Distribution*
✔ *The Gamma Distribution*
✔ *The Beta Distribution*
✔ *The Chi-Square Distribution*
✔ *Student's t Distribution*
✔ *The F Distribution*
✔ *Relationships Among Chi-Square, t, and F Distributions*

The Multinomial Distribution

Suppose that events $A_1, A_2, \ldots, A_k$ are mutually exclusive, and can occur with respective probabilities $p_1, p_2, \ldots, p_k$ where $p_1 + p_2 + \cdots + p_k + 1$. If $X_1, X_2, \ldots, X_k$ are the random variables, respectively, giving the number of times that $A_1, A_2, \ldots, A_k$ occur in a total of n trials, so that $X_1 + X_2 + \cdots X_k = n$, then

$$P(X_1 = n_1, X_2 = n_2, \ldots, X_k = n_k) = \frac{n}{n_1! n_2! \cdots n_k!} p_1^{n_1} p_2^{n_k} \cdots p_k^{n_k} \quad (1)$$

where $n_1 + n_2 + \cdots n_k = n$, is the joint probability function for the random variables $X_1, X_2, \ldots, X_k$.

This distribution, which is a generalization of the binomial distribution, is called the *multinomial distribution* since the equation above is the general term in the multinomial expansion of $(p_1 + p_2 + \cdots p_k)^n$.

The Hypergeometric Distribution

Suppose that a box contains b blue marbles and r red marbles. Let us perform n trials of an experiment in which a marble is chosen at random, its color observed, and then the marble is put back in the box. This type of experiment is often referred to as *sampling with replacement*. In such a case, if X is the random variable denoting the number of blue marbles chosen (successes) in n trials, then using the binomial distribution we see that the probability of exactly x successes is

$$P(X = x) = \binom{n}{x} \frac{b^x r^{n-x}}{(b+r)^n}, \qquad x = 0, 1, \ldots, n \quad (2)$$

since $p = b/(b+r), q = 1 - p = r/(b+r)$.

If we modify the above so that *sampling is without replacement,* i.e., the marbles are not replaced after being chosen, then

$$P(X = x) = \frac{\binom{b}{x}\binom{r}{n-x}}{\binom{b+r}{n}}, \quad x = \max(0, n - r),..., \min(n,b) \quad (3)$$

This is the *hypergeometric distribution.* The mean and variance for this distribution are

$$\mu = \frac{nb}{b+r}, \quad \sigma^2 = \frac{nbr(b+r-n)}{(b+r)^2(b+r-1)} \quad (4)$$

If we let the total number of blue and red marbles be N, while the proportions of blue and red marbles are p and $q = 1 - p$, respectively, then

$$p = \frac{b}{b+r} = \frac{b}{N}, \quad q = \frac{r}{b+r} = \frac{r}{N} \quad \text{or} \quad b - Np, \quad r = Nq$$

This leads us to the following

$$P(X = x) = \frac{\binom{Np}{x}\binom{Nq}{n-x}}{\binom{N}{n}} \quad (5)$$

$$\mu = np, \quad \sigma^2 = \frac{npq(N-n)}{N-1} \quad (6)$$

Note that as $N \to \infty$ (or N is large when compared with n), these two formulas reduce to the following

$$P(X = x) = \binom{n}{x} p^x q^{n-x} \qquad (7)$$

$$\mu = np, \qquad \sigma^2 = npq \qquad (8)$$

Notice that this is the same as the mean and variance for the binomial distribution. The results are just what we would expect, since for large N, sampling without replacement is practically identical to sampling with replacement.

Example 10.1 A box contains 6 blue marbles and 4 red marbles. An experiment is performed in which a marble is chosen at random and its color is observed, but the marble is not replaced. Find the probability that after 5 trials of the experiment, 3 blue marbles will have been chosen.

The number of different ways of selecting 3 blue marbles out of 6 marbles is $\binom{6}{3}$. The number of different ways of selecting the remaining 2 marbles out of the 4 red marbles is $\binom{4}{2}$. Therefore, the number of different samples containing 3 blue marbles and 2 red marbles is $\binom{6}{3}\binom{4}{2}$.

Now the total number of different ways of selecting 5 marbles out of the 10 marbles (6 + 4) in the box is $\binom{10}{5}$. Therefore, the required probability is given by

$$\frac{\binom{6}{3}\binom{4}{2}}{\binom{10}{5}} = \frac{10}{21}$$

The Uniform Distribution

A random variable X is said to be *uniformly distributed* in $a \leq x \leq b$ if its density function is

$$f(x) = \begin{cases} 1/(b-a) & a \leq x \leq b \\ 0 & otherwise \end{cases} \tag{9}$$

and the distribution is called a *uniform distribution*.
    The distribution function is given by

$$F(x) = P(X \leq x) = \begin{cases} 0 & x < a \\ (x-a)/(b-a) & a \leq x < b \\ 1 & x \geq b \end{cases} \tag{10}$$

The mean and variance are, respectively

$$\mu = \frac{1}{2}(a+b), \qquad \sigma^2 = \frac{1}{12}(b-a)^2 \tag{11}$$

The Cauchy Distribution

A random variable X is said to be *Cauchy distributed*, or to have the *Cauchy distribution*, if the density function of X is

$$f(x) = \frac{a}{\pi(x^2 + a^2)} \qquad a > 0, -\infty < x < \infty \tag{12}$$

The density function is symmetrical about $x = 0$ so that its median is zero. However, the mean and variance do not exist.

The Gamma Distribution

A random variable X is said to have the *gamma distribution*, or to be *gamma distributed*, if the density function is

$$f(x) = \begin{cases} \dfrac{x^{\alpha-1}e^{-x/\beta}}{\beta^{\alpha}\Gamma(\alpha)} & x > 0 \\ 0 & x \le 0 \end{cases} \qquad (\alpha, \beta > 0) \tag{13}$$

where $\Gamma(\alpha)$ is the *gamma function* (see Appendix A). The mean and variance are given by

$$\mu = \alpha\beta \qquad \sigma^2 = \alpha\beta^2 \tag{14}$$

The Beta Distribution

A random variable is said to have the *beta distribution*, or to be *beta distributed*, if the density function is

$$f(x) = \begin{cases} \dfrac{x^{\alpha-1}(1-x)^{\beta-1}}{B(\alpha, \beta)} & 0 < x < 1 \\ 0 & \text{otherwise} \end{cases} \qquad (\alpha, \beta > 0) \tag{15}$$

where $B(\alpha, \beta)$ is the *beta function* (see Appendix A). In view of the relation between the beta and gamma functions, the beta distribution can also be defined by the density function

$$f(x) = \begin{cases} \dfrac{\Gamma(\alpha+\beta)}{\Gamma(\alpha)\Gamma(\beta)} x^{\alpha-1}(1-x)^{\beta-1} & 0 < x < 1 \\[3mm] 0 & \text{otherwise} \end{cases} \qquad (16)$$

where α, β are positive. The mean and variance are

$$\mu = \frac{\alpha}{\alpha+\beta}, \quad \sigma^2 = \frac{\alpha\beta}{(\alpha+\beta)^2(\alpha+\beta+1)} \qquad (17)$$

For $\alpha > 1$, $\beta > 1$ there is a unique mode at the value

$$x_{\text{mode}} = \frac{\alpha-1}{\alpha+\beta-2} \qquad (18)$$

The Chi-Square Distribution

Let X_1, X_2, ...,X_ν be ν independent normally distributed random variables with mean zero and variance one. Consider the random variable

$$\chi^2 = X_1^2 + X_2^2 + \cdots + X_\nu^2 \qquad (19)$$

where χ^2 is called *chi square*. Then we can show that for all $x \geq 0$,

$$P(\chi^2 \le x) = \frac{1}{2^{v/2}\Gamma(v/2)} \int_0^x u^{(v/2)-1} e^{-u/2} \, du \qquad (20)$$

and $P(\chi^2 \le x) = 0$ for $x > 0$.

The distribution above is called the *chi-square distribution*, and v is called the *number of degrees of freedom*. The distribution defined above has corresponding density function given by

$$f(x) = \begin{cases} \dfrac{1}{2^{v/2}\Gamma(v/2)} x^{(v/2)-1} e^{-x/2} & x > 0 \\ \\ 0 & x \le 0 \end{cases} \qquad (21)$$

It is seen that the chi-square distribution is a special case of the gamma distribution with $\alpha = v/2$ and $\beta = 2$. Therefore,

$$\mu = v, \qquad \sigma^2 = 2v \qquad (22)$$

For large v $(v \ge 30)$, we can show that $\sqrt{2\chi^2} - \sqrt{2v-1}$ is very nearly normally distributed with mean 0 and variance one.

Three theorems that will be useful in later work are as follows:

Theorem 10-1: Let X_1, X_2, ..., X_v be independent normally random variables with mean 0 and variance 1. Then $\chi^2 = X_1^2 + X_2^2 + \cdots + X_v^2$ is chi square distributed with v degrees of freedom.

Theorem 10-2: Let U_1, U_2, ..., U_k be independent random variables that are chi square distributed with v_1, v_2, ..., v_k degrees of freedom, respectively. Then their sum $W = U_1 + U_2 + \cdots U_k$ is chi square distributed with $v_1 + v_2 + \cdots v_k$ degrees of freedom.

Theorem 10-3: Let V_1 and V_2 be independent random variables. Suppose that V_1 is chi square distributed with v_1 degrees of freedom while $V = V_1 = V_2$ is chi square distributed with v degrees of freedom, where $v > v_1$. Then V_2 is chi square distributed with $v - v_1$ degrees of freedom.

In connection with the chi-square distribution, the t distribution, the F distribution, and others, it is common in statistical work to use the *same symbol* for both the random variable and a value of the random variable. Therefore, percentile values of the chi-square distribution for v degrees of freedom are denoted by $\chi^2_{p,v}$, or briefly χ^2_p if v is understood, and not by $\chi^2_{p,v}$ or x_p. (See Appendix D.) This is an ambiguous notation, and the reader should use care with it, especially when changing variables in density functions.

Example 10.2. The graph of the chi-square distribution with 5 degrees of freedom is shown in Figure 10-1. Find the values for χ^2_1, χ^2_2 for which the shaded area on the right $= 0.05$ and the total shaded area $= 0.05$.

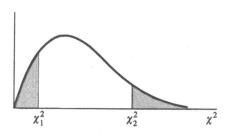

Figure 10-1

If the shaded area on the right is 0.05, then the area to the left of χ_2^2 is

$(1 - 0.05) = 0.95$, and χ_2^2 represents the 95th percentile, $\chi_{0.95}^2$.

Referring to the table in Appendix D, proceed downward under the column headed v until entry 5 is reached. Then proceed right to the column headed $\chi_{0.95}^2$. The result, 11.1, is the required value of χ^2.

Secondly, since the distribution is not symmetric, there are many values for which the total shaded area $= 0.05$. For example, the right-handed shaded area could be 0.04 while the left-handed area is 0.01. It is customary, however, unless otherwise specified, to choose the two areas equal. In this case, then, each area $= 0.025$.

If the shaded area on the right is 0.025, the area to the left of χ_2^2 is

$1 - 0.025 = 0.975$ and χ_2^2 represents the 97.5th percentile $\chi_{0.975}^2$, which from Appendix D is 12.8.

Similarly, if the shaded area on the left is 0.025, the area to the left of χ_1^2 is 0.025 and χ_1^2 represents the 2.5th percentile, $\chi_{0.025}^2$, which equals 0.831.

Therefore, the values are 0.831 and 12.8.

Student's *t* Distribution

If a random variable has the density function

$$f(t) = \frac{\Gamma\left(\dfrac{v+1}{2}\right)}{\sqrt{v\pi}\ \Gamma\left(\dfrac{v}{2}\right)}\left(1 + \frac{t^2}{v}\right)^{-(v+1)/2} \qquad -\infty < t < \infty \qquad (23)$$

it is said to have the *Student's t distribution*, briefly the *t distribution*, with v degrees of freedom. If v is large ($v \geq 30$), the graph of $f(t)$ closely approximates the normal curve, as indicated in Figure 10-2.

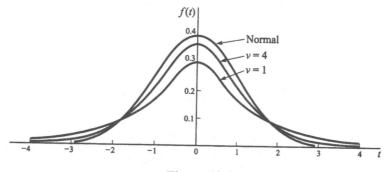

Figure 10-2

Percentile values of the t distribution for v degrees of freedom are denoted by $t_{p,v}$ or briefly t_p if v is understood. For a table giving such values, see Appendix C. Since the t distribution is symmetrical, $t_{1-p} = -t_p$; for example, $t_{0.5} = -t_{0.95}$.

For the t distribution we have

$$\mu = 0 \qquad \text{and} \qquad \sigma^2 = \frac{v}{v-2} \qquad (v > 2) \qquad (24)$$

The following theorem is important in later work.

Theorem 10-4: Let Y and Z be independent random variables, where Y is normally distributed with mean 0 and variance 1 while Z is chi square distributed with v degrees of freedom. Then the random variable

$$T = \frac{Y}{\sqrt{Z/v}}$$

(25)

has the t distribution with v degrees of freedom.

Example 10.3. The graph of Student's *t distribution* with 9 degrees of freedom is shown in Figure 10-3. Find the value of t_1 for which the shaded area on the right = 0.05 and the total unshaded area = 0.99.

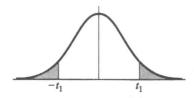

Figure 10-3

If the shaded area on the right is 0.05, then the area to the left of t_1 is (1 − 0.05) = 0.095, and t_1 represents the 95th percentile, $t_{0.95}$. Referring to the table in Appendix C, proceed downward under the column headed v until entry 9 is reached. Then proceed right to the column headed $t_{0.95}$. The result 1.83 is the required value of *t*.

Next, if the total unshaded area is 0.99, then the total shaded area is (1 − 0.99) = 0.01, and the shaded area to the right is 0.01 / 2 = 0.005. From the table we find $t_{0.995} = 3.25$.

The *F* Distribution

A random variable is said to have the *F* distribution (named after R. A. Fisher) with v_1 and v_2 *degrees of freedom* if its density function is given by

$$f(u) = \begin{cases} \dfrac{\Gamma\left(\dfrac{v_1 + v_2}{2}\right)}{\Gamma\left(\dfrac{v_1}{2}\right)\Gamma\left(\dfrac{v_2}{2}\right)} v_1^{v_1/2} v_2^{v_2/2} u^{(v_1/2)-1} (v_2 + v_1 u)^{-(v_1+v_2)/2} & u > 0 \\ \\ 0 & u \le 0 \end{cases} \tag{26}$$

Percentile values of the F distribution for v_1, v_2 degrees of freedom are denoted by $F_{p,v1,v2}$, or briefly F_p if v_1 and v_2 are understood.

For a table giving such values in the case where $p = 0.95$ and $p = 0.99$, see Appendix E.

The mean and variance are given, respectively, by

$$\mu = \frac{v_2}{v_2 - 2} \quad (v_2 > 2) \quad \text{and} \quad \sigma^2 = \frac{2v_2^2(v_1 + v_2 + 2)}{v_1(v_2 - 4)(v_2 - 2)^2} \quad (27)$$

The distribution has a unique mode at the value

$$u_{mode} = \left(\frac{v_1 - 2}{v_1}\right)\left(\frac{v_2}{v_2 + 2}\right) \quad (v_1 > 2) \quad (28)$$

The following theorems are important in later work.

Theorem 11-5: Let V_1 and V_2 be independent random variables that are chi square distributed with v_1 and v_2 degrees of freedom, respectively. Then the random variable

$$V = \frac{V_1 / v_1}{V_2 / v_2} \quad (29)$$

has the F distribution with v_1 and v_2 degrees of freedom.

Theorem 10-6:
$$F_{1-p,v_2,v_1} = \frac{1}{F_{p,v_1,v_2}} \quad (30)$$

> ## Remember
>
> While specially used with small samples, Student's t distribution, the chi-square distribution, and the F distribution are all valid for large sample sizes as well.

Relationships Among Chi-Square, t, and F Distributions

Theorem 10-7:
$$F_{1-p,1,v} = t^2_{1-(p/2),v} \qquad (31)$$

Theorem 10-8:
$$F_{p,v,\infty} = \frac{\chi^2_{p,v}}{v} \qquad (32)$$

Example 10.4. Verify Theorem 10-7 by showing that $F_{0.95} = t^2_{0.975}$.

Compare the entries in the first column of the $F_{0.95}$ table in Appendix E with those in the t distribution under $t_{0.975}$. We see that

$$161 = (12.71)^2, \quad 18.5 = (4.30)^2, \quad 10.1 = (3.18)^2, \quad 7.71 = (2.78)^2, \text{ etc.,}$$

which provides the required verification.

Example 10.5. Verify Theorem 10-8 for $p = 0.99$.

Compare the entries in the last row of the $F_{0.99}$ table in Appendix E (corresponding to $v_2 = \infty$) with the entries under $\chi^2_{0.99}$ in Appendix D. Then we see that

$$6.63 = \frac{6.63}{1}, \quad 4.61 = \frac{9.21}{2}, \quad 3.78 = \frac{11.3}{3}, \quad 3.32 = \frac{13.3}{4}, \text{ etc.,}$$

which provides the required verification.

Appendix A

Mathematical Topics

Special Sums

The following are some of the sums of series that arise in practice. By definition, $0! = 1$. Where the series is infinite, the range of convergence is indicated.

1. $\displaystyle\sum_{j=1}^{m} j = 1+2+3+\cdots+m = \frac{m(m+1)}{2}$

2. $\displaystyle\sum_{j=1}^{m} j^2 = 1^2+2^2+3^2+\cdots m^2 = \frac{m(m+1)(2m+1)}{6}$

3. $\displaystyle e^x = 1+x+\frac{x^2}{2!}+\frac{x^3}{3!}+\cdots = \sum_{j=0}^{\infty} \frac{x^j}{j!}$ all x

4. $\displaystyle \sin x = x-\frac{x^3}{3!}+\frac{x^5}{5!}-\frac{x^7}{7!}+\cdots = \sum_{j=0}^{\infty} \frac{(-1)^j x^{2j+1}}{(2j+1)!}$ all x

5. $\displaystyle \cos x = 1-\frac{x^2}{2!}+\frac{x^4}{4!}-\frac{x^6}{6!}+\cdots = \sum_{j=0}^{\infty} \frac{(-1)^j x^{2j}}{(2j)!}$ all x

6. $\displaystyle \frac{1}{1-x} = 1+x+x^2+x^3+\cdots = \sum_{j=0}^{\infty} x^j$ $|x|<1$

7. $\displaystyle \ln(1-x) = -x-\frac{x^2}{2}-\frac{x^3}{3}-\frac{x^4}{4}-\cdots = -\sum_{j=1}^{\infty} \frac{x^j}{j}$ $-1 \le x < 1$

Eulers' Formulas

8. $e^{i\theta} = \cos\theta + i\sin\theta$, $\qquad e^{-i\theta} = \cos\theta - i\sin\theta$

9. $\cos\theta = \dfrac{e^{i\theta} + e^{-i\theta}}{2}$, $\qquad \sin\theta = \dfrac{e^{i\theta} - e^{-i\theta}}{2i}$

The Gamma Function

The *gamma function*, denoted by $\Gamma(n)$ is denoted by

$$\Gamma(n) = \int_0^\infty t^{n-1} e^{-t}\, dt \qquad n > 0$$

A *recurrence formula* is given by

$$\Gamma(n+1) = n\Gamma(n)$$

where $\Gamma(1) = 1$. An extension of the gamma function to $n < 0$ can be obtained by use of the recurrence function above.

If n is a positive integer, then

$$\Gamma(n+1) = n!$$

For this reason $\Gamma(n)$ sometimes called the *factorial function*. An important property of the gamma function is that

$$\Gamma(p)\Gamma(1-p) = \frac{\pi}{\sin p\pi}$$

For $p = \dfrac{1}{2}$, this gives

$$\Gamma\left(\frac{1}{2}\right) = \sqrt{\pi}$$

For large values of n we have *Stirling's asymptotic formula:*

$$\Gamma(n+1) \sim \sqrt{2\pi n} n^n e^{-n}$$

The Beta Function

The *beta function*, denoted by $B(m, n)$, is defined as

$$B(m,n) = \int_0^1 u^{m-1}(1-u)^{n-1}\, du \quad m > 0, n > 0$$

It is related to the gamma function by

$$B(m,n) = \frac{\Gamma(m)\Gamma(n)}{\Gamma(m+n)}$$

Special Integrals

10. $\displaystyle \int_0^\infty e^{-ax^2}\, dx = \frac{1}{2}\sqrt{\frac{\pi}{a}} \qquad a > 0$

11. $\displaystyle \int_0^\infty x^m e^{-ax^2}\, dx = \frac{\Gamma\left(\dfrac{m+1}{2}\right)}{2a^{(m+1)/2}} \qquad a > 0,\ m > -1$

12. $\displaystyle \int_0^\infty e^{-ax^2} \cos bx\, dx = \frac{1}{2}\sqrt{\frac{\pi}{a}}\, e^{-b^2/4a} \qquad a > 0$

13. $\displaystyle \int_0^\infty e^{-ax} \cos bx\, dx = \frac{a}{a^2 + b^2} \qquad a > 0$

14. $\displaystyle \int_0^\infty e^{-ax} \sin bx\, dx = \frac{b}{a^2 + b^2} \qquad a > 0$

15. $\displaystyle\int_0^\infty x^{p-1}e^{-ax}\,dx = \frac{\Gamma(p)}{a^p}$ $a>0, p>0$

16. $\displaystyle\int_{-\infty}^\infty e^{-(ax^2+bx+c)}\,dx = \sqrt{\frac{\pi}{a}}\,e^{(b^2-4ac)/4a}$ $a>0$

17. $\displaystyle\int_0^\infty e^{-(ax^2+bx+c)}\,dx = \frac{1}{2}\sqrt{\frac{\pi}{a}}\,e^{(b^2-4ac)/4a}\,\mathrm{erfc}\!\left(\frac{b}{2\sqrt{a}}\right)$ $a>0$

where

$$erfc(u) = 1 - erf(u) = 1 - \frac{2}{\sqrt{\pi}}\int_0^u e^{-x^2}\,dx = \frac{2}{\sqrt{\pi}}\int_u^\infty e^{-x^2}\,dx$$

is called the *complementary error function*.

18. $\displaystyle\int_0^\infty \frac{\cos\omega x}{x^2+a^2}\,dx = \frac{\pi}{2a}e^{-a\omega}$ $a>0, \omega>0$

19. $\displaystyle\int_0^{\pi/2} \sin^{2m-1}\theta\cos^{2n-1}\theta\,d\theta = \frac{\Gamma(m)\Gamma(n)}{2\Gamma(m+n)}$ $m>0, n$

Appendix B

Areas under the Standard Normal Curve from 0 to z

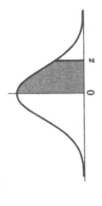

z	0	1	2	3	4	5	6	7	8	9
0.0	.0000	.0040	.0080	.0120	.0160	.0199	.0239	.0279	.0319	.0359
0.1	.0398	.0438	.0478	.0517	.0557	.0596	.0636	.0675	.0714	.0754
0.2	.0793	.0832	.0871	.0910	.0948	.0987	.1026	.1064	.1103	.1141
0.3	.1179	.1217	.1255	.1293	.1331	.1368	.1406	.1443	.1480	.1517
0.4	.1554	.1591	.1628	.1664	.1700	.1736	.1772	.1808	.1844	.1879
0.5	.1915	.1950	.1985	.2019	.2054	.2088	.2123	.2157	.2190	.2224
0.6	.2258	.2291	.2324	.2357	.2389	.2422	.2454	.2486	.2518	.2549
0.7	.2580	.2612	.2642	.2673	.2704	.2734	.2764	.2794	.2823	.2852
0.8	.2881	.2910	.2939	.2967	.2996	.3023	.3051	.3078	.3106	.3133
0.9	.3159	.3186	.3212	.3238	.3264	.3289	.3315	.3340	.3365	.3389
1.0	.3413	.3438	.3461	.3485	.3508	.3531	.3554	.3577	.3599	.3621
1.1	.3643	.3665	.3686	.3708	.3729	.3749	.3770	.3790	.3810	.3830
1.2	.3849	.3869	.3888	.3907	.3925	.3944	.3962	.3980	.3997	.4015
1.3	.4032	.4049	.4066	.4082	.4099	.4115	.4131	.4147	.4162	.4177
1.4	.4192	.4207	.4222	.4236	.4251	.4265	.4279	.4292	.4306	.4319

z	.00	.01	.02	.03	.04	.05	.06	.07	.08	.09
1.5	.4332	.4345	.4357	.4370	.4382	.4394	.4406	.4418	.4429	.4441
1.6	.4452	.4463	.4474	.4484	.4495	.4505	.4515	.4525	.4535	.4545
1.7	.4554	.4564	.4573	.4582	.4591	.4599	.4608	.4616	.4625	.4633
1.8	.4641	.4649	.4656	.4664	.4671	.4678	.4686	.4693	.4699	.4706
1.9	.4713	.4719	.4726	.4732	.4738	.4744	.4750	.4756	.4761	.4767
2.0	.4772	.4778	.4783	.4788	.4793	.4798	.4803	.4808	.4812	.4817
2.1	.4821	.4826	.4830	.4834	.4838	.4842	.4846	.4850	.4854	.4857
2.2	.4861	.4864	.4868	.4871	.4875	.4878	.4881	.4884	.4887	.4890
2.3	.4893	.4896	.4898	.4901	.4904	.4906	.4909	.4911	.4913	.4916
2.4	.4918	.4920	.4922	.4925	.4927	.4929	.4931	.4932	.4934	.4936
2.5	.4938	.4940	.4941	.4943	.4945	.4946	.4948	.4949	.4951	.4952
2.6	.4953	.4955	.4956	.4957	.4959	.4960	.4961	.4962	.4963	.4964
2.7	.4965	.4966	.4967	.4968	.4969	.4970	.4971	.4972	.4973	.4974
2.8	.4974	.4975	.4976	.4977	.4977	.4978	.4979	.4979	.4980	.4981
2.9	.4981	.4982	.4982	.4983	.4984	.4984	.4985	.4985	.4986	.4986
3.0	.4987	.4987	.4987	.4988	.4988	.4989	.4989	.4989	.4990	.4990
3.1	.4990	.4991	.4991	.4991	.4992	.4992	.4992	.4992	.4993	.4993
3.2	.4993	.4993	.4994	.4994	.4994	.4994	.4994	.4995	.4995	.4995
3.3	.4995	.4995	.4995	.4996	.4996	.4996	.4996	.4996	.4996	.4997
3.4	.4997	.4997	.4997	.4997	.4997	.4997	.4997	.4997	.4997	.4998
3.5	.4998	.4998	.4998	.4998	.4998	.4998	.4998	.4998	.4998	.4998
3.6	.4998	.4998	.4999	.4999	.4999	.4999	.4999	.4999	.4999	.4999
3.7	.4999	.4999	.4999	.4999	.4999	.4999	.4999	.4999	.4999	.4999
3.8	.4999	.4999	.4999	.4999	.4999	.4999	.4999	.4999	.4999	.4999
3.9	.5000	.5000	.5000	.5000	.5000	.5000	.5000	.5000	.5000	.5000

Appendix C

Student's *t* Distribution

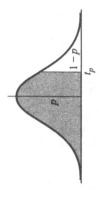

ν	$t_{.55}$	$t_{.60}$	$t_{.70}$	$t_{.75}$	$t_{.80}$	$t_{.90}$	$t_{.95}$	$t_{.975}$	$t_{.99}$	$t_{.995}$
1	.158	.325	.727	1.000	1.376	3.08	6.31	12.71	31.82	63.66
2	.142	.289	.617	.816	1.061	1.89	2.92	4.30	6.96	9.92
3	.137	.277	.584	.765	.978	1.64	2.35	3.18	4.54	5.84
4	.134	.271	.569	.741	.941	1.53	2.13	2.78	3.75	4.60
5	.132	.267	.559	.727	.920	1.48	2.02	2.57	3.36	4.03
6	.131	.265	.553	.718	.906	1.44	1.94	2.45	3.14	3.71
7	.130	.263	.549	.711	.896	1.42	1.90	2.36	3.00	3.50
8	.130	.262	.546	.706	.889	1.40	1.86	2.31	2.90	3.36
9	.129	.261	.543	.703	.883	1.38	1.83	2.26	2.82	3.25
10	.129	.260	.542	.700	.879	1.37	1.81	2.23	2.76	3.17
11	.129	.260	.540	.697	.876	1.36	1.80	2.20	2.72	3.11
12	.128	.259	.539	.695	.873	1.36	1.78	2.18	2.68	3.06

df										
13	3.01	2.65	2.16	1.77	1.35	.870	.694	.538	.259	.128
14	2.98	2.62	2.14	1.76	1.34	.868	.692	.537	.258	.128
15	2.95	2.60	2.13	1.75	1.34	.866	.691	.536	.258	.128
16	2.92	2.58	2.12	1.75	1.34	.865	.690	.535	.258	.128
17	2.90	2.57	2.11	1.74	1.33	.863	.689	.534	.257	.128
18	2.88	2.55	2.10	1.73	1.33	.862	.688	.534	.257	.127
19	2.86	2.54	2.09	1.73	1.33	.861	.688	.533	.257	.127
20	2.84	2.53	2.09	1.72	1.32	.860	.687	.533	.257	.127
21	2.83	2.52	2.08	1.72	1.32	.859	.686	.532	.257	.127
22	2.82	2.51	2.07	1.72	1.32	.858	.686	.532	.256	.127
23	2.81	2.50	2.07	1.71	1.32	.858	.685	.532	.256	.127
24	2.80	2.49	2.06	1.71	1.32	.857	.685	.531	.256	.127
25	2.79	2.48	2.06	1.71	1.32	.856	.684	.531	.256	.127
26	2.78	2.48	2.06	1.71	1.32	.856	.684	.531	.256	.127
27	2.77	2.47	2.05	1.70	1.31	.855	.684	.531	.256	.127
28	2.76	2.47	2.05	1.70	1.31	.855	.683	.530	.256	.127
29	2.76	2.46	2.04	1.70	1.31	.854	.683	.530	.256	.127
30	2.75	2.46	2.04	1.70	1.31	.854	.683	.530	.256	.127
40	2.70	2.42	2.02	1.68	1.30	.851	.681	.529	.255	.126
60	2.66	2.39	2.00	1.67	1.30	.848	.679	.527	.254	.126
120	2.62	2.36	1.98	1.66	1.29	.845	.677	.526	.254	.126
∞	2.58	2.33	1.96	1.645	1.28	.842	.674	.524	.253	.126

Appendix D

Chi-Square Distribution

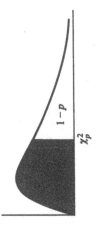

ν	$\chi^2_{.005}$	$\chi^2_{.01}$	$\chi^2_{.025}$	$\chi^2_{.05}$	$\chi^2_{.10}$	$\chi^2_{.25}$	$\chi^2_{.50}$	$\chi^2_{.75}$	$\chi^2_{.90}$	$\chi^2_{.95}$	$\chi^2_{.975}$	$\chi^2_{.99}$	$\chi^2_{.995}$	$\chi^2_{.999}$
1	.0000	.0002	.0010	.0039	.0158	.102	.455	1.32	2.71	3.84	5.02	6.63	7.88	10.8
2	.0100	.0201	.0506	.103	.211	.575	1.39	2.77	4.61	5.99	7.38	9.21	10.6	13.8
3	.0717	.115	.216	.352	.584	1.21	2.37	4.11	6.25	7.81	9.35	11.3	12.8	16.3
4	.207	.297	.484	.711	1.06	1.92	3.36	5.39	7.78	9.49	11.1	13.3	14.9	18.5
5	.412	.554	.831	1.15	1.61	2.67	4.35	6.63	9.24	11.1	12.8	15.1	16.7	20.5
6	.676	.872	1.24	1.64	2.20	3.45	5.35	7.84	10.6	12.6	14.4	16.8	18.5	22.5
7	.989	1.24	1.69	2.17	2.83	4.25	6.35	9.04	12.0	14.1	16.0	18.5	20.3	24.3
8	1.34	1.65	2.18	2.73	3.49	5.07	7.34	10.2	13.4	15.5	17.5	20.1	22.0	26.1
9	1.73	2.09	2.70	3.33	4.17	5.90	8.34	11.4	14.7	16.9	19.0	21.7	23.6	27.9
10	2.16	2.56	3.25	3.94	4.87	6.74	9.34	12.5	16.0	18.3	20.5	23.2	25.2	29.6
11	2.60	3.05	3.82	4.57	5.58	7.58	10.3	13.7	17.3	19.7	21.9	24.7	26.8	31.3
12	3.07	3.57	4.40	5.23	6.30	8.44	11.3	14.8	18.5	21.0	23.3	26.2	28.3	32.9

df														
13	3.57	4.11	5.01	5.89	7.04	9.30	12.3	16.0	19.8	22.4	24.7	27.7	29.8	34.5
14	4.07	4.66	5.63	6.57	7.79	10.2	13.3	17.1	21.1	23.7	26.1	29.1	31.3	36.1
15	4.60	5.23	6.26	7.26	8.55	11.0	14.3	18.2	22.3	25.0	27.5	30.6	32.8	37.7
16	5.14	5.81	6.91	7.96	9.31	11.9	15.3	19.4	23.5	26.3	28.8	32.0	34.3	39.3
17	5.70	6.41	7.56	8.67	10.1	12.8	16.3	20.5	24.8	27.6	30.2	33.4	35.7	40.8
18	6.26	7.01	8.23	9.39	10.9	13.7	17.3	21.6	26.0	28.9	31.5	34.8	37.2	42.3
19	6.84	7.63	8.91	10.1	11.7	14.6	18.3	22.7	27.2	30.1	32.9	36.2	38.6	43.8
20	7.43	8.26	9.59	10.9	12.4	15.5	19.3	23.8	28.4	31.4	34.2	37.6	40.0	45.3
21	8.03	8.90	10.3	11.6	13.2	16.3	20.3	24.9	29.6	32.7	35.5	38.9	41.4	46.8
22	8.64	9.54	11.0	12.3	14.0	17.2	21.3	26.0	30.8	33.9	36.8	40.3	42.8	48.3
23	9.26	10.2	11.7	13.1	14.8	18.1	22.3	27.1	32.0	35.2	38.1	41.6	44.2	49.7
24	9.89	10.9	12.4	13.8	15.7	19.0	23.3	28.2	33.2	36.4	39.4	43.0	45.6	51.2
25	10.5	11.5	13.1	14.6	16.5	19.9	24.3	29.3	34.4	37.7	40.6	44.3	46.9	52.6
26	11.2	12.2	13.8	15.4	17.3	20.8	25.3	30.4	35.6	38.9	41.9	45.6	48.3	54.1
27	11.8	12.9	14.6	16.2	18.1	21.7	26.3	31.5	36.7	40.1	43.2	47.0	49.6	55.5
28	12.5	13.6	15.3	16.9	18.9	22.7	27.3	32.6	37.9	41.3	44.5	48.3	51.0	56.9
29	13.1	14.3	16.0	17.7	19.8	23.6	28.3	33.7	39.1	42.6	45.7	49.6	52.3	58.3
30	13.8	15.0	16.8	18.5	20.6	24.5	29.3	34.8	40.3	43.8	47.0	50.9	53.7	59.7
40	20.7	22.2	24.4	26.5	29.1	33.7	39.3	45.6	51.8	55.8	59.3	63.7	66.8	73.4
50	28.0	29.7	32.4	34.8	37.7	42.9	49.3	56.3	63.2	67.5	71.4	76.2	79.5	86.7
60	35.5	37.5	40.5	43.2	46.5	52.3	59.3	67.0	74.4	79.1	83.3	88.4	92.0	99.6
70	43.3	45.4	48.8	51.7	55.3	61.7	69.3	77.6	85.5	90.5	95.0	100	104	112
80	51.2	53.5	57.2	60.4	64.3	71.1	79.3	88.1	96.6	102	107	112	116	125
90	59.2	61.8	65.6	69.1	73.3	80.6	89.3	98.6	108	113	118	124	128	137
100	67.3	70.1	74.2	77.9	82.4	90.1	99.3	109	118	124	130	136	140	149

Appendix E

95th and 99th Percentile Values for the F Distribution

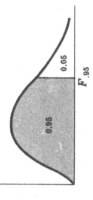

$F_{.95}$

v_1 / v_2	1	2	3	4	5	6	7	8	9	10	12	15	20	24	30	40	60	120	∞
1	161	200	216	225	230	234	237	239	241	242	244	246	248	249	250	251	252	253	254
2	18.5	19.0	19.2	19.2	19.3	19.3	19.4	19.4	19.4	19.4	19.4	19.4	19.4	19.5	19.5	19.5	19.5	19.5	19.5
3	10.1	9.55	9.28	9.12	9.01	8.94	8.89	8.85	8.81	8.79	8.74	8.70	8.66	8.64	8.62	8.59	8.57	8.55	8.53
4	7.71	6.94	6.59	6.39	6.26	6.16	6.09	6.04	6.00	5.96	5.91	5.86	5.80	5.77	5.75	5.72	5.69	5.66	5.63
5	6.61	5.79	5.41	5.19	5.05	4.95	4.88	4.82	4.77	4.74	4.68	4.62	4.56	4.53	4.50	4.46	4.43	4.40	4.37
6	5.99	5.14	4.76	4.53	4.39	4.28	4.21	4.15	4.10	4.06	4.00	3.94	3.87	3.84	3.81	3.77	3.74	3.70	3.67
7	5.59	4.74	4.35	4.12	3.97	3.87	3.79	3.73	3.68	3.64	3.57	3.51	3.44	3.41	3.38	3.34	3.30	3.27	3.23
8	5.32	4.46	4.07	3.84	3.69	3.58	3.50	3.44	3.39	3.35	3.28	3.22	3.15	3.12	3.08	3.04	3.01	2.97	2.93
9	5.12	4.26	3.86	3.63	3.48	3.37	3.29	3.23	3.18	3.14	3.07	3.01	2.94	2.90	2.86	2.83	2.79	2.75	2.71
10	4.96	4.10	3.71	3.48	3.33	3.22	3.14	3.07	3.02	2.98	2.91	2.85	2.77	2.74	2.70	2.66	2.62	2.58	2.54
11	4.84	3.98	3.59	3.36	3.20	3.09	3.01	2.95	2.90	2.85	2.79	2.72	2.65	2.61	2.57	2.53	2.49	2.45	2.40
12	4.75	3.89	3.49	3.26	3.11	3.00	2.91	2.85	2.80	2.75	2.69	2.62	2.54	2.51	2.47	2.43	2.38	2.34	2.30
13	4.67	3.81	3.41	3.18	3.03	2.92	2.83	2.77	2.71	2.67	2.60	2.53	2.46	2.42	2.38	2.34	2.30	2.25	2.21
14	4.60	3.74	3.34	3.11	2.96	2.85	2.76	2.70	2.65	2.60	2.53	2.46	2.39	2.35	2.31	2.27	2.22	2.18	2.13

15	2.07	2.11	2.16	2.20	2.25	2.29	2.33	2.40	2.48	2.54	2.59	2.64	2.71	2.79	2.90	3.06	3.29	3.68	4.54
16	2.01	2.06	2.11	2.15	2.19	2.24	2.28	2.35	2.42	2.49	2.54	2.59	2.66	2.74	2.85	3.01	3.24	3.63	4.49
17	1.96	2.01	2.06	2.10	2.15	2.19	2.23	2.31	2.38	2.45	2.49	2.55	2.61	2.70	2.81	2.96	3.20	3.59	4.45
18	1.92	1.97	2.02	2.06	2.11	2.15	2.19	2.27	2.34	2.41	2.46	2.51	2.58	2.66	2.77	2.93	3.16	3.55	4.41
19	1.88	1.93	1.98	2.03	2.07	2.11	2.16	2.23	2.31	2.38	2.42	2.48	2.54	2.63	2.74	2.90	3.13	3.52	4.38
20	1.84	1.90	1.95	1.99	2.04	2.08	2.12	2.20	2.28	2.35	2.39	2.45	2.51	2.60	2.71	2.87	3.10	3.49	4.35
21	1.81	1.87	1.92	1.96	2.01	2.05	2.10	2.18	2.25	2.32	2.37	2.42	2.49	2.57	2.68	2.84	3.07	3.47	4.32
22	1.78	1.84	1.89	1.94	1.98	2.03	2.07	2.15	2.23	2.30	2.34	2.40	2.46	2.55	2.66	2.82	3.05	3.44	4.30
23	1.76	1.81	1.86	1.91	1.96	2.01	2.05	2.13	2.20	2.27	2.32	2.37	2.44	2.53	2.64	2.80	3.03	3.42	4.28
24	1.73	1.79	1.84	1.89	1.94	1.98	2.03	2.11	2.18	2.25	2.30	2.36	2.42	2.51	2.62	2.78	3.01	3.40	4.26
25	1.71	1.77	1.82	1.87	1.92	1.96	2.01	2.09	2.16	2.24	2.28	2.34	2.40	2.49	2.60	2.76	2.99	3.39	4.24
26	1.69	1.75	1.80	1.85	1.90	1.95	1.99	2.07	2.15	2.22	2.27	2.32	2.39	2.47	2.59	2.74	2.98	3.37	4.23
27	1.67	1.73	1.79	1.84	1.88	1.93	1.97	2.06	2.13	2.20	2.25	2.31	2.37	2.46	2.57	2.73	2.96	3.35	4.21
28	1.65	1.71	1.77	1.82	1.87	1.91	1.96	2.04	2.12	2.19	2.24	2.29	2.36	2.45	2.56	2.71	2.95	3.34	4.20
29	1.64	1.70	1.75	1.81	1.85	1.90	1.94	2.03	2.10	2.18	2.22	2.28	2.35	2.43	2.55	2.70	2.93	3.33	4.18
30	1.62	1.68	1.74	1.79	1.84	1.89	1.93	2.01	2.09	2.16	2.21	2.27	2.33	2.42	2.53	2.69	2.92	3.32	4.17
40	1.51	1.58	1.64	1.69	1.74	1.79	1.84	1.92	2.00	2.08	2.12	2.18	2.25	2.34	2.45	2.61	2.84	3.23	4.08
60	1.39	1.47	1.53	1.59	1.65	1.70	1.75	1.84	1.92	1.99	2.04	2.10	2.17	2.25	2.37	2.53	2.76	3.15	4.00
120	1.25	1.35	1.43	1.50	1.55	1.61	1.66	1.75	1.83	1.91	1.96	2.02	2.09	2.18	2.29	2.45	2.68	3.07	3.92
∞	1.00	1.22	1.32	1.39	1.46	1.52	1.57	1.67	1.75	1.83	1.88	1.94	2.01	2.10	2.21	2.37	2.60	3.00	3.84

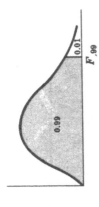

$F_{.99}$

ν_2 \ ν_1	1	2	3	4	5	6	7	8	9	10	12	15	20	24	30	40	60	120	∞
1	4052	5000	5403	5625	5764	5859	5928	5981	6023	6056	6106	6157	6209	6235	6261	6287	6313	6339	6366
2	98.5	99.0	99.2	99.2	99.3	99.3	99.4	99.4	99.4	99.4	99.4	99.4	99.4	99.5	99.5	99.5	99.5	99.5	99.5
3	34.1	30.8	29.5	28.7	28.2	27.9	27.7	27.5	27.3	27.2	27.1	26.9	26.7	26.6	26.5	26.4	26.3	26.2	26.1
4	21.2	18.0	16.7	16.0	15.5	15.2	15.0	14.8	14.7	14.5	14.4	14.2	14.0	13.9	13.8	13.7	13.7	13.6	13.5
5	16.3	13.3	12.1	11.4	11.0	10.7	10.5	10.3	10.2	10.1	9.89	9.72	9.55	9.47	9.38	9.29	9.20	9.11	9.02
6	13.7	10.9	9.78	9.15	8.75	8.47	8.26	8.10	7.98	7.87	7.72	7.56	7.40	7.31	7.23	7.14	7.06	6.97	6.88
7	12.2	9.55	8.45	7.85	7.46	7.19	6.99	6.84	6.72	6.62	6.47	6.31	6.16	6.07	5.99	5.91	5.82	5.74	5.65
8	11.3	8.65	7.59	7.01	6.63	6.37	6.18	6.03	5.91	5.81	5.67	5.52	5.36	5.28	5.20	5.12	5.03	4.95	4.86
9	10.6	8.02	6.99	6.42	6.06	5.80	5.61	5.47	5.35	5.26	5.11	4.96	4.81	4.73	4.65	4.57	4.48	4.40	4.31
10	10.0	7.56	6.55	5.99	5.64	5.39	5.20	5.06	4.94	4.85	4.71	4.56	4.41	4.33	4.25	4.17	4.08	4.00	3.91
11	9.65	7.21	6.22	5.67	5.32	5.07	4.89	4.74	4.63	4.54	4.40	4.25	4.10	4.02	3.94	3.86	3.78	3.69	3.60
12	9.33	6.93	5.95	5.41	5.06	4.82	4.64	4.50	4.39	4.30	4.16	4.01	3.86	3.78	3.70	3.62	3.54	3.45	3.36
13	9.07	6.70	5.74	5.21	4.86	4.62	4.44	4.30	4.19	4.10	3.96	3.82	3.66	3.59	3.51	3.43	3.34	3.25	3.17

14	3.00	3.09	3.18	3.27	3.35	3.43	3.51	3.66	3.80	3.94	4.03	4.14	4.28	4.46	4.70	5.04	5.56	6.51	8.86
15	2.87	2.96	3.05	3.13	3.21	3.29	3.37	3.52	3.67	3.80	3.89	4.00	4.14	4.32	4.56	4.89	5.42	6.36	8.68
16	2.75	2.84	2.93	3.02	3.10	3.18	3.26	3.41	3.55	3.69	3.78	3.89	4.03	4.20	4.44	4.77	5.29	6.23	8.53
17	2.65	2.75	2.83	2.92	3.00	3.08	3.16	3.31	3.46	3.59	3.68	3.79	3.93	4.10	4.34	4.67	5.19	6.11	8.40
18	2.57	2.66	2.75	2.84	2.92	3.00	3.08	3.23	3.37	3.51	3.60	3.71	3.84	4.01	4.25	4.58	5.09	6.01	8.29
19	2.49	2.58	2.67	2.76	2.84	2.92	3.00	3.15	3.30	3.43	3.52	3.63	3.77	3.94	4.17	4.50	5.01	5.93	8.18
20	2.42	2.52	2.61	2.69	2.78	2.86	2.94	3.09	3.23	3.37	3.46	3.56	3.70	3.87	4.10	4.43	4.94	5.85	8.10
21	2.36	2.46	2.55	2.64	2.72	2.80	2.88	3.03	3.17	3.31	3.40	3.51	3.64	3.81	4.04	4.37	4.87	5.78	8.02
22	2.31	2.40	2.50	2.58	2.67	2.75	2.83	2.98	3.12	3.26	3.35	3.45	3.59	3.76	3.99	4.31	4.82	5.72	7.95
23	2.26	2.35	2.45	2.54	2.62	2.70	2.78	2.93	3.07	3.21	3.30	3.41	3.54	3.71	3.94	4.26	4.76	5.66	7.88
24	2.21	2.31	2.40	2.49	2.58	2.66	2.74	2.89	3.03	3.17	3.26	3.36	3.50	3.67	3.90	4.22	4.72	5.61	7.82
25	2.17	2.27	2.36	2.45	2.54	2.62	2.70	2.85	2.99	3.13	3.22	3.32	3.46	3.63	3.86	4.18	4.68	5.57	7.77
26	2.13	2.23	2.33	2.42	2.50	2.58	2.66	2.82	2.96	3.09	3.18	3.29	3.42	3.59	3.82	4.14	4.64	5.53	7.72
27	2.10	2.20	2.29	2.38	2.47	2.55	2.63	2.78	2.93	3.06	3.15	3.26	3.39	3.56	3.78	4.11	4.60	5.49	7.68
28	2.06	2.17	2.26	2.35	2.44	2.52	2.60	2.75	2.90	3.03	3.12	3.23	3.36	3.53	3.75	4.07	4.57	5.45	7.64
29	2.03	2.14	2.23	2.33	2.41	2.49	2.57	2.73	2.87	3.00	3.09	3.20	3.33	3.50	3.73	4.04	4.54	5.42	7.60
30	2.01	2.11	2.21	2.30	2.39	2.47	2.55	2.70	2.84	2.98	3.07	3.17	3.30	3.47	3.70	4.02	4.51	5.39	7.56
40	1.80	1.92	2.02	2.11	2.20	2.29	2.37	2.52	2.66	2.80	2.89	2.99	3.12	3.29	3.51	3.83	4.31	5.18	7.31
60	1.60	1.73	1.84	1.94	2.03	2.12	2.20	2.35	2.50	2.63	2.72	2.82	2.95	3.12	3.34	3.65	4.13	4.98	7.08
120	1.38	1.53	1.66	1.76	1.86	1.95	2.03	2.19	2.34	2.47	2.56	2.66	2.79	2.96	3.17	3.48	3.95	4.79	6.85
∞	1.00	1.32	1.47	1.59	1.70	1.79	1.88	2.04	2.18	2.32	2.41	2.51	2.64	2.80	3.02	3.32	3.78	4.61	6.63

Appendix F

Values of $e^{-\lambda}$

$(0 < \lambda < 1)$

λ	0	1	2	3	4	5	6	7	8	9
0.0	1.0000	.9900	.9802	.9704	.9608	.9512	.9418	.9324	.9231	.9139
0.1	.9048	.8958	.8869	.8781	.8694	.8607	.8521	.8437	.8353	.8270
0.2	.8187	.8106	.8025	.7945	.7866	.7788	.7711	.7634	.7558	.7483
0.3	.7408	.7334	.7261	.7189	.7118	.7047	.6977	.6907	.6839	.6771
0.4	.6703	.6636	.6570	.6505	.6440	.6376	.6313	.6250	.6188	.6126
0.5	.6065	.6005	.5945	.5886	.5827	.5770	.5712	.5655	.5599	.5543
0.6	.5488	.5434	.5379	.5326	.5273	.5220	.5169	.5117	.5066	.5016
0.7	.4966	.4916	.4868	.4819	.4771	.4724	.4677	.4630	.4584	.4538
0.8	.4493	.4449	.4404	.4360	.4317	.4274	.4232	.4190	.4148	.4107
0.9	.4066	.4025	.3985	.3946	.3906	.3867	.3829	.3791	.3753	.3716

$$(\lambda = 1, 2, 3, \ldots, 10)$$

λ	1	2	3	4	5	6	7	8	9	10
$e^{-\lambda}$	.36788	.13534	.04979	.01832	.006738	.002479	.000912	.000335	.000123	.000045

NOTE: To obtain values of $e^{-\lambda}$ for other values of λ, use the laws of exponents.

Example: $e^{-3.48} = (e^{-3.00})(e^{-0.48}) = (.04979)(.6188) = .03081$.

Appendix G

Random Numbers

51772	74640	42331	29044	46621	62898	93582	04186	19640	87056
24033	23491	83587	06568	21960	21387	76105	10863	97453	90581
45939	60173	52078	25424	11645	55870	56974	37428	93507	94271
30586	02133	75797	45406	31041	86707	12973	17169	88116	42187
03585	79353	81938	82322	96799	85659	36081	50884	14070	74950
64937	03355	95863	20790	65304	55189	00745	65253	11822	15804
15630	64759	51135	98527	62586	41889	25439	88036	24034	67283
09448	56301	57683	30277	94623	85418	68829	06652	41982	49159
21631	91157	77331	60710	52290	16835	48653	71590	16159	14676
91097	17480	29414	06829	87843	28195	27279	47152	35683	47280

Index